THE 10 WAYS
TO
LIVE BETTER

Discover How to Improve Your Lifestyle, How to Build Strong Relationships to Live Better and Work on Your Mindset to Change Your Habits

Raymond Harold

Table of Contents

Chapter 1 First Things First 1

Chapter 2 The First On The First Things First List: Spirituality . 34

Chapter 3 Understanding The How To Deal With Money 44

Chapter 4 The Underrated Value Of Family 48

Chapter 5 The Misunderstood Meaning Of: Self Love 55

Chapter 6 Mastering Our Own Soul Through: Exercise 68

Chapter 7 The Selfless Act Of: Giving Back 72

Chapter 8 Mastering The Body And Soul Through: Relaxation .. 79

Chapter 9 Controlling What Controls People: Fear 88

Chapter 10 Communication: As A Means Of Relation 100

Chapter 11 Loving What Earns You A Living: Job 113

Chapter 12 The Final Chapter: Live!!! 126

Chapter 1
First Things First

It seems to be remarkably easy to fall into unhealthy routines.

- Eating junk food.
- Watching TV instead of going to the gym.
- Showing up to a job you hate every day.
- Biting your nails.
- Smoking.

There is no lack of unhealthful and unproductive conduct. And from moment to moment, we're all fighting with them. But why is it? You're trying to live a nice, fulfilling and beautiful life. And you're likely really motivated and inspired to create a change every now and then. So how come next year you're more likely to do the same thing than do something better? Why is it so difficult to stick to healthy habits? I believe it's because we're usually trying to make changes in the wrong way. And in this guide, I'm going to share a combination of science and real-world experiences that share a better attitude to making long-term changes to your life.

Let's get started.

The Common Mistake You Want to Avoid

Your audacious life goals are fabulous. We're proud of you for having them. But it's possible that those goals are designed to distract you from the thing that's really frightening you—the shift in daily habits that would mean a re–invention of how you see yourself.—Seth Godin

Transformations and overnight achievements are going to get a lot of hype. (For good reason, who wouldn't want to be more effective in less time?) But here's the issue: when you hear about a drastic transition (like someone losing 100 pounds) or an incredible success story (like someone building a million-dollar company in a year), the only thing you understand is the event individuals talk about. You don't hear anything about the process that went before it, or about the practices that led to the final outcome.

It's simple to let those incredible tales trick you into doing too much, too quickly. I understand I did it. When you're motivated and inspired to bring your life to the next level, it's so simple to get obsessed with the consequence. I've got to lose 20 pounds (or 40 or 60 or 100). I need to squat 300 pounds (or 400 or 500 pounds). I need 3 days of meditation a week (or 5 or 7). Or thousands of other differences in your life objectives.

It's natural to believe that we need an outcome, a transformation, a success overnight. But that's not exactly what you need. You need to have better practices. It is so simple to overestimate the significance of a defining time and underestimate the value of making better choices on a daily basis. Almost every habit you have— good or bad — is the consequence of many tiny choices over time. And if this is true, if the problems you face now are the result of thousands of small choices made over the years, wouldn't it make sense that the route to achievement, health, strength, happiness, satisfaction, significance, and vitality would also be through thousands of daily decisions? And yet, how easy it is to forget this when we want to create a shift. When you're obsessed with getting an outcome rapidly, the only thing you're thinking about is how to get to your objective, and you forget to understand that our goal-making method is just as crucial as to whether or not you're going to accomplish it. The desire to obtain outcomes rapidly fools you into believing that the award is the outcome.

But here's the truth…

The type of person you want to be— someone who lives to a stronger standard, who is convinced of itself and who can be counted on by the people who are important to them— is the daily process through which you pass, not the ultimate product through which you pass. Why is it true, huh? Because, basically, life today is the sum of your habits. How are you out of shape? Well, this is because of your own practice. How pleased or unhappy are you about this? Well, this is because of your own practice. How successful or unsuccessful have you been in that? Well, this is because of your own practice.

What you do repeatedly (i.e. what you spend your time thinking and doing every day) ultimately forms the person that you are, the things you believe in, and the personality that you portray. The most common mistake people make is to focus on the situation, the conversion, the overnight success they want to achieve –rather than focusing on their activities and routines. Like everyone else, I was guilty of this. And still today, I'm learning how to master your own methods.

But over time, I have found a useful combination of academic studies and real-world experience that has allowed me to make progress in many areas of life. In this guide, I would like to share this progress with you so that you can avoid chasing another success overnight and actually stick to your long-term goals.

Let's get started by talking about the science of sticking to good habits.

The Science of How Your Habits Work

(The 3 R's of Habit Change)

There is a simple 3–step pattern that every habit follows. I call this pattern the

"3 R's of Habit Change" and it goes like this...

1. Reminder (the trigger that initiates the behavior)
2. Routine (the behavior itself; the action you take)
3. Reward (the benefit you gain from doing the behavior)

This sequence has been constantly demonstrated by behavioral psychologists. At the start, I learned about this cycle from Stanford Professor BJ Fogg.

More recently, Charles Duping in the best-selling book The Power of Habit. (The Duping book refers to the three steps as a cue, a routine and a reward. Whatever it says, behind the habit formation technique there is a lot of knowledge, which means that we may be relatively confident that you will be in a similar way.) (If you answer a telephone call)

Step One: Your phone rings (reminder). This is a reminder that triggers conduct. The ring acts as an indicator to tell you to reply to the telephone. It is the time that the behavior begins.

Step Two: You answer your phone (routine). This is the actual behavior. You have a habit of answering when your phone rings.

Step Three: You find out who is calling (reward). You will find out who calls (reward). The benefit of the behavior is the reward. In this case, your curiosity about why the other person called for you was satisfied with the price for completed the habits.

Result: If the reward is good, the cycle forms a favorable feedback loop that says to your brain, "Do the same thing next time this reminder occurs."

You'd stop thinking about it. Follow this same cycle enough times. Your conduct is just going to become a habit. The same three-step process forms all practices.

How can this structure be used to build and adhere to new habits?

Here's how…

Step 1: Talking to you about a new habit with your colleagues could tell you that you need self-control, or you have to discover a new dose of goodwill. Use your new one with your current habits as a reminder.

I disagree.

It is the exact wrong way to get motivated and remember a new behavior. It's meaningful if you think of it. You feel motivated sometimes and you don't, right, sometimes? Why would you like to rely on motivation (something that changes) to create a new custom (something you want)?

This is why it is such a crucial component of creating new habits–the trigger of your new conduct. A nice reminder makes it simpler for you to begin your habit by encrypting your fresh behavior, instead of motivating yourself.

For instance, after breaking my teeth, I have developed a fresh habit of flossing every day. I already did the act of brushing my teeth and it was the cause or indication of my fresh conduct.

I purchased a bowl, set it beside my toothbrush, and put in there a couple of previous-made flowers to make things even easier and stop myself from having to remember flossing. Now each time I reach my toothbrush, I see the floss.

It was much simpler to modify by establishing a visible reminder, connecting my new habits to present behavior. There must be no motivation. You don't have to remember that.

How to Choose Your Reminder

Whether it works, eats healthily, or builds art does not matter, you can't magically expect to adhere to another habit without a scheme that makes starting much easier. And that is why it is the first step to make change easier to choose the right reminders for your new habits.

It is your life and habits to remember that you are attempting to start your fresh behavior.

The best thing I know is to write down two lists to remember your fresh habits. Write the things you do every day in the first list without fail.

- For example...
- Get in the shower.
- Put your shoes on.
- Brush your teeth.
- Flush the toilet.
- Sit down for dinner.
- Turn the lights off.
- Get into bed.

Many of these things are daily healthy habits, including washing your face, drinking morning tea, brushing your teeth, etc. you will often discover. These measures may serve as a reminder of fresh health behaviors. For instance, "I meditate for 60 seconds after I drink tea in the morning."

In the second list, write down the things that happen to you each day...

- You stop at a red light.
- You get a text message.

- A commercial comes on TV.
- A song ends.
- The sun sets.

These events may also trigger your new habits. For example, if you want to "I make five pushups when you get a commercial on TV," you'll have two lists of different things that you already are doing and that you're responding to every day. You have two lists. These reminders are perfect for new habits. Let's say, for instance, that you want to feel better. Thankfulness is a proven way to enhance happiness. Using the above list, you can select "Sit for dinner" from the record and use it to say one thing you are gratefully appreciative of today. "One thing I say when I sit down for dinner today I'm thankful for." That's the kind of small behavior that might flourish to give a more thankful perspective on life in the main.

Step 2: Make Your Habits Incredibly Easy to Start

Make it so easy you can't say no.—Leo Babauta

As noted at the start of this guide, the desire to make huge changes in your lives is unbelievably simple to catch. We are watching incredible changes in weight loss and believe that in the next four weeks we need to lose 30 pounds. We're seeing elite TV athletes and want to go quicker tomorrow and jump quicker. Right now, we want to get more, do more and be more. Those stuff, too, I've felt, so I get it. I applaud enthusiasm in general. I'm happy that for your life you want excellent stuff, and I want to do everything I can to assist you do them. However, it should be remembered that enduring change is the result of daily behaviors, not changes once in a lifetime.

If you would like to begin a new habit and start to live fitter and happier, then I've got one suggestion I cannot focus enough: start little. From the words of Leo Babauta,"make it so simple that you cannot say no more."

How little? Stanford professor BJ Fogg indicates that individuals who wish to begin flossing start by flossing just 1 tooth. Just one.

Initially, performance does not matter. It's possible to build up to the amount of functionality which you would like when the behavior gets constant. Your homework: Select a brand new habit that you would like to begin. Ask yourself, "How do I create this new behavior really simple to do I cannot say no?"

Step 3: Always Reward Yourself

It is very important to observe. (I believe that is as true in life as it's with customs.)

If it comes to adhering to better customs, there's a significant motive to always reward yourself: we would like to keep on doing things which make us feel great. And that's the reason it's particularly important that you reward yourself every time you exercise your new habit.

By way of instance, if I am working towards a new exercise goal, then I will often tell myself in the end of a work out, "This has been a good day." Or, "Great job. You made progress now." If you really feel like it, you may even tell yourself "Victory!" Every time you do your own new habit.

- Floss one tooth. "Victory!"
- Eat a healthy meal. "Success!"
- Do five pushups. "Good work!"

Rewarding yourself with self-Speak could take some getting used to if you are not somebody who typically does this. But even though it seems absurd, studies have demonstrated that the benefit is a significant part the habit procedure. Related note: Be certain the customs you're working to build are really important for you. It is hard to discover a reward in something when you are just doing this because you think other men and women anticipate it or might approve of it. It is your own life, so be certain that you're spending your time on matters which are important for you. Now that we have covered the science of habit formation, let us discuss how to utilize it in actual life. Identity-Based Habits: How to Really Follow Your Goals for Your Long-Term.

But in the actual world, there's frequently a gap between practice and theory. Whenever I write, I do my very best not to only share thoughts backed by mathematics, but also to emphasize real-world courses which make it much easier for you to place those thoughts into practice.

This is particularly important in regards to building better customs. We All need to become better individuals -- fitter and stronger, more innovative and more proficient, a much better friend or relative. But if we get very inspired and begin doing things better, it is hard to really adhere to new behaviors. It is more probable this time you'll do exactly the exact same thing than doing a new habit easily.

Here's how it works...

What Remembering Names Can Teach You About Habits

My girlfriend is very good at remembering people's names. Recently, she told me a story that occurred when she was at high school. She moved into a large high school, and it was the very first day of course. A number of the pupils had never met before that afternoon. The instructor moved across the room and asked each individual to introduce themselves. In the conclusion, the instructor asked if anyone can remember everybody's name.

My girlfriend raised her hands and proceeded to move round the area and correctly name all 30 or so individuals. The remainder of the area was stunned. The man beside her appeared and said, "I could not even remember your name" Then happened, she felt just like, "I am the kind of person who's capable of remembering people's names".

Even today, she's excellent at remembering the names of anybody we encounter. Here is what I heard from this story: To be able to trust in a fresh identity, we must prove ourselves.

Identity-Based Habits: How to Build Lasting Habits

Your existing behaviors are only a manifestation of your present identity.

To change your behavior permanently, you have to begin believing new things on your own.

Envision the way we typically set aims. We may begin with stating "I wish to get rid of weight" or "I need to get more powerful." If you are lucky, somebody may say, "That is fantastic, but you ought to be more specific.".

These goals are based around our physical appearance.

Performance and look goals are fantastic, but they are not exactly the same as customs. If you are doing a behavior, then these kinds of goals will help push you ahead. But if you are attempting to initiate a new behavior, I think that it would be much better to begin with an identity--established goal.

The inside of behavior change and constructing better customs is the individuality. Each action you are doing is driven by the basic belief it is possible. Therefore, in the event that you change your individuality (the kind of individual that you feel you are), then it is a lot easier to change your own actions.

The main reason it's so tough to abide by new customs is that we frequently attempt to attain a performance or look --established goal without altering our individuality. It must be the other way round.

The Recipe for Sustained Success

Changing your beliefs isn't nearly as hard as you might think. There are two steps.

1. Decide the type of person you want to be.
2. Prove it to yourself with small wins.

Note: I cannot emphasize enough how important It's to start with incredibly small measures. The objective isn't to achieve results at first, the objective is to develop into the type of person who can attain these things.

By Way of Example, a person who works out regularly is the type of individual who can become strong? Develop the identity of somebody who works out first, and then proceed to performance and appearance later. Start small and hope that the results will come because you develop a new identity. On the next page, you'll locate five examples of how you can use identity-based habits in real life.

Example 1: Want to lose weight?

Identity: Become the kind of individual who moves more every day.

Small win: get a pedometer. When you get back from job, walk 50 steps.

Tomorrow, go 100 steps. The next day, 150 steps. If you do this 5 days a week and add 50 steps a day, then by the end of the year, you'll be walking more than 10,000 steps a day.

Example 2: Do you want to become a better writer?

Identity: Become the sort of individual who writes 1,000 words each day.

Small Win: Write one paragraph every day of the week.

Example 3: Do you want to be powerful?

Identity: Become the kind of individual who never misses a workout.

Small win: Do push-ups every Monday, Wednesday and Friday.

Example 4: Would you like to be a better friend?

Identity: Become a sort of individual who is always in contact.

Small win: call a friend every Saturday. If you repeat the same individuals every three months, you'll remain close to 12 ancient friends all year round.

Example 5: Do you want to be taken seriously at job?

Identity: become the sort of individual who's always on time.

Small win: schedule meetings with an extra 15-minute gap between them so that you can go from conference to conference and always show up early.

What is your identity?

This is especially true in the beginning.

Should you would like to get motivated and inspired, then do not hesitate to see a YouTube video, listen to a favorite song, or try P90X. But do not be amazed if you burn out after a week. You can't count on being encouraged to make lasting changes in your life. You have to develop into the sort of person that you need to be, which begins with proving your identity to yourself.

If you are looking to create a change, I say quit worrying about results and begin worrying about your identity. Become the type of individual who will reach the things that you want to achieve. Construct the habit today. The outcomes can come after.

Combining Strategies for Maximum Success.

Identity-based habits offer you a frame by which to see your own objectives. The three R's of dependency change provides a plan for attaining your identity. Combining these two notions will create change easier for you overall.

To put it differently, identity-based habits keep you focused on the right things: like starting little, building your individuality, instead of worrying about results.

Meanwhile, the three R's of dependence shift ensure you do matters in an ideal way: just like linking your new habit to current behavior and rewarding to work well done.

The Perfect Way to Start Your Own New Habit

If you're seriously considering doing things better than you are now -- in other words, even if you are intent on adhering to good habits -- then you've got to start small.

Envision the standard habits, good or bad: Brushing your teeth. Putting your seatbelt on. Biting your nails.

You merely do them automatically. They are miniature activities that become constant patterns.

Would not it make sense that when we wanted to form new habits, the very best way to begin would be to make tiny changes which our mind could quickly learn and mechanically replicate?

Imagine if you started thinking of your life objectives, much less big, audacious matters that you might only achieve when the time is right or when you have greater funds or whenever you finally catch your big break... but instead as tiny, daily behaviors which are repeated till success becomes inevitable? .

Imagine if losing 50 pounds wasn't determined by research discovering the ideal diet plan or you locate a superhuman dose of willpower, but hinged into a string of small customs that you may consistently restrain? Habits such as walking for 20 minutes daily, drinking 8 glasses of water daily, eating two meals rather than three.

Too frequently we get obsessed with creating life-changing transformations. I think you'd make more improvement by focusing on lifestyle behaviors.

- Losing 50 pounds could be drinking 8 glasses of water daily is a new kind of lifestyle.
- Running a marathon would be life-changing, going an additional five hours a week as a freelancer is a whole new kind of lifestyle.
- Publishing your first book could be life-changing, exposing a brand new publication representative daily is a new kind of lifestyle.
- Earning an additional $20,000 annually could be life-changing, working an additional five hours a week for a freelancer is a new sort of lifestyle.

Can you find the difference?

Should you plant the ideal seed in the ideal place, it is going to grow without further afield. I feel that is the ideal metaphor for producing habits.

The "correct seed" is your very small behavior which you pick. The "right place" is your sequencing -- exactly what it comes later. The "coaxing" component is making upward motivation, which I believe has nothing to do with producing customs.

Allow me to be explicit: If you decide on the ideal little behavior and order it correctly, then you certainly won't need to motivate yourself to get it grow. It is going to only happen naturally, such as a fantastic seed planted at a fantastic place.

How great is that?

Typically, as soon as you receive a dose of motivation, you will go into the deep just to fail rapidly and would like your fresh habit to drown out more willingness. The fresh strategy is to wade deeper into the shallow waters until you can swim, regardless of your motivation.

Daily habits— small and repeatable routines — are the realities of great dreams. Big dream, but tiny beginning.

How to fit your life with new habits.

One thing is to know how to change, but it is completely different to fit fresh objectives in your lives.

It's hard to make modifications. Whenever your timetable gets insane, life's inertia can take you away from your objectives and back into your old habits.

How can you overcome this tendency to drop and to create time on your timetable for fresh objectives?

Using the policies already listed in this guide, such as 3 R's of change in habits and identity, will assist you to follow through.

But the only instruments at your disposal are these strategies. I will share a different way to stick to healthy habits which require no incredible amount of willpower or notable motivation. in this chapter. Two examples will also be shared of how I have effectively used that approach in my own life.

The issue is how we normally set objectives.

You have dreams and goals in your life if you are anything like the typical human being. Indeed, you likely want to achieve many stuff— big and small.

That's fantastic, but we often make a prevalent error in setting objectives. (I understand that many times I committed myself this mistake).

The issue is: we set a time limit but not a timetable.

We concentrate on our final objective and the deadline by which we are going to accomplish it. We say things like, "In the summer I want to lose 20 livres," or "In the next 12 weeks, I will add 50 pounds to my bench press."

The issue with this approach is that if we fail to accomplish our initial arbitrary time frame, we feel like we're failing... even though we're better off than we were at the beginning. Sadly, the end outcome is that we often give up if the original date does not achieve our target.

The excellent news is here: better and easy. Here is the excellent news.

The power to set a timetable, not a time limit.

In my experience, it is more effective to establish a timetable to work than a deadline for achieving your objectives and building healthy practices.

Instead of offering yourself a time limit to fulfill a specific objective (and feel like a breakdown if you do not achieve that), you must select an objective that is essential to you.

That might not sound like a major shift, but it is.

Most of the moment, I attempt to practice my thoughts, not just to express my views, so let me use two true examples of my own life to explain the approach.

Example 1: Writing

Each Monday and Thursday, I release a fresh post. I have delivered two papers every week, each week since my first post on 12 November 2012.

The post is sometimes less than anticipated, sometimes less convincing than I had hoped, and sometimes less helpful than it could be... but it nevertheless reaches out to the globe.

Naturally, I haven't always operated on a program on Monday / Thursday. Actually, I found reasons to avoid a timetable actively. I informed myself, "I write my best, when I am inspired, and I just wait for the urge to write." I informed myself.

I assumed I shouldn't do it at all if I didn't do my best work. This strategy's issue is that my production was at best irregular. It took me time to do this, but it doesn't always have to do your best, it is to do the best that you can on a coherent basis.

Once I stopped concentrating on outcomes and simply kept to a coherent timetable, I enhanced my job and my performance. I wrote more in amount and better in quality than in the past two years in the first 6 months following my start writing two times a week.

It doesn't matter what you do, if you just work if you feel driven, you will never be sufficiently coherent to influence your life significantly.

Example 2: Exercise.

I chose to push up 100 pushups in a string in rigorous shape in August 2012. I only received 36 when I first attempted it.

In the past, I could have set myself a deadline: "Do 100 pushups by 31st December."

I decided this time to set an appointment timetable. Every Monday, Wednesday and Friday I began doing pushup training. For any exercise, there was no complete push-up objective. The aim is to do the training merely. (As for no article that I write, there is no single objective. The purpose is to write the article merely).

In the nine months that have followed me since my start, I maintained my timetable Monday, Wednesday, and Friday and finished more than 100 pushup workouts. I'm still on my manner to 100 successive pushups (My present best is 80 a row).

Concentrate on the practice, not the achievement.

See how the two above examples differ from most of our objectives?

In both instances (writing and training), I have consistently advanced my objectives not by setting my performance deadlines, but by following a timetable. The emphasis is not on the achievement of the X target by a given date.

If you want to be the kind of person who does things consistently, give yourself a schedule, not a deadline to go.

How can big changes be made without being overwhelmed?

I am a great advocate to do one thing at a moment. There is a lot of studies that shows that it is less profitable than to remain focused on one objective to multiple tasks and divide your attention. However, what if in your lives you want to make several changes? What if, at more than one thing, you want to get home... and you want to? Well, I have fine news. Through "keystone habits," you can concentrate on one thing and simultaneously enhance your life in a number of fields.

Let's discuss what key habits are and how in your lives you can use them.

The Power of Keystone Habits

One of the primary customs, of course, is a conduct that attracts the rest of your life so that you can hear it in the book of Charles Duhigg, The Power of the Habit. When I began to look at my own lives, I began to observe some routines that resulted in better behavior.

When I'm training, I want to eat healthier. I can reward myself with ice cream and chocolate bars, but I like good food without processing. When I start working after practice, I seem to be more effective. Ideas are flowing easily.

And at the end of the day, I fall asleep quickly. I tend to sleep and feel cool when I wake up.

If I don't exercise, I see the opposite impact. On irrelevant tasks, I remain up and distracted and waste time. There is increasing stress and tension in my back.

Fitness is the primary exercise which brings together the remainder of my life, to put it differently. I don't believe about any better food. I have no obligation to concentrate on doing things.

I'm not always at the top of my game, but when I train, everything looks a bit simpler. Exercise of course leads me to my best.

What Are Your Keystone Habits?

Enhancing your lifestyle and getting the sort of person that "has their act together" is not quite as difficult as you may think. In reality, you may need only 1 keystone habit prior to the dominoes start falling anywhere.

In case you've got several things you want to enhance, imagine how much easier it will be that you do if you found just one or two keystone habits that obviously set you on the road to achievement.

The great news? You most likely already know these behaviors are for you personally.

What's the 1 thing which -- when you get it done -- your day appears to go more easily?

For me personally, it's exercising. Meanwhile, other men and women swear from the dawn run. And you will discover heaps of CEOs who assert their everyday meditation habit would be the secret to their achievement.

Regardless of what your own keystone dependency is, it's worth your time to concentrate on it and do much more of it. The ideal dependence, when done regularly, can affect your life in a lot of ways.

How to Get Back on Track After Slipping Up

The formation of habit depends on your capacity to rebound. There will always be instances when it is fundamentally not feasible to follow your ordinary routine.

But small hops don't make you fail, they make you personally. In their customs also the most affluent people on the planet rush up. It's not their ability to avoid mistakes that characterizes them, but their abilities to rapidly get back on track.

The main point to be seen is that the best approach is not to avoid failure, but that it is to plan. Using the four approaches you can develop a "strategy for madness" and a plan before you get away.

1. Put your habits on your calendar.

Claiming that you want to accomplish vague goals (i.e., "I want to eat healthfully") is not a clear program for your ideas to operate.

Your customs take time and place to live on.

Want to get back on the correct path with your program of writing? Seat cable. Seat cable. Hands on keyboard. Hands-on. That's when this happens.

Would you like to practice? I'm going to see you in the gym.

The most significant thing is: it may be good to tell you that you will probably change, but becoming special makes it real and gives you a reason to go back on the correct path as you slide up.

There's no time soon, and some aren't a number. Where and when are you supposed to do this, exactly? Have you set up a scheme to remind you of your fresh customization?

Note: The best way to "remind yourself automatically" is merely to link your fresh person to your existing behavior.

2. Even in small respects, stick on your program. This is not the individual effect of slipping away. It is the cumulative impact of not returning to the correct path. (i.e. It is important to follow your program for this reason, although it is only in very small terms.

- Do you not have time for a full exercise? Just squat.
- Don't you have enough time for a post to write? Write a paragraph.
- Are you not having enough time for yoga? 10 seconds to breathe.
- Are you not having enough time on vacation? Drive to the nearby town, take a mini-break.

Find a way, however small, of adhering to the program. Another example is here... Another instance...

Say you woke up this afternoon for up to 3 miles today. During the day, your schedule was crazy and it started to flee. When you look at the clock, you only have 20 minutes to train.

At this point, you have two options.

You will probably be convinced that it is preferable to take your time to contact e-mailed or make a postponed phone call... Or another thousand alternatives. You can probably take the time to do this.

That is what I'd done in the past, get time pressed and don't work for a good reason.

Secondly, it reduces its scope, but it is necessary to keep to the schedule. You could say to yourself, "We're not 20 minutes in time for change, but it's time for my shoes to go and 5 sprints" Every day it doesn't really affect you, especially when you're 3 miles long. But it always has an enormous cumulative effect on time.

Moreover, this strategy allows you to prove yourself that you can do something, even if the situation is not ideal. The long-lasting success is always the cumulative effects that will comply with your schedule.

This is how small goals become life's habits.

3. Have someone waiting for you.

I've been on many teams during my athletic career. You know how you expect your friends, teammates and coaches to practice? You show up. You show up. You show up. You show up.

The good news is you don't need to work with a team. Talk to foreigners and make friends at the gym. I only know you can be happy that a familiar face is looking forward to seeing you.

4. Design your environment to be successful.

If you think you want more motivation or more readiness to stick to your goals, I have great news. You do not. You do not. You just don't. You just don't.

Most of us accept that the people around us have an impact on our behavior, but we know less about the connection between our behavior.

The truth is, the signs you read, the things on your desk, the images on your walls in the building all make you feel motivated, and that you can do something different.

One of the most important changes, when I wanted to constantly begin to slit, was to remove the flour from the tubing and keep it on my counter next to my tooth bow. It sounds like a dumb thing to focus on, however, because of the visual clue that I saw each time I burnt my teeth I didn't have to remember to remove it from the drawer,

This simple environment change made it easy for me to make a new habit and no more willingness or motivation was necessary.

Develop a Plan for Bouncing Back

Change can be difficult. You could begin by two steps forward and one step back from your healthy habits. Preventing these measures backwards and creating a plan for rapid progress can create a difference in the globe.

How to Break a Bad Habit (and Replace it With a Good One)

We talked a lot about how good habits can be made, but what about breaking the bad ones?

Bad habits disturb your life and stop your objectives from being reached.

Their health is mentally as well as physically dangerous. You have lost your time and power. So why do we continue to do so? And above all, can you do something about it? How can we eliminate good conduct and maintain it?

Of course, I don't have all the answers, but I will keep reading and sharing my lessons about bad habits.

What causes bad habits?

Two things are mostly triggered by your bad habits...

Boredom and Stress.

Bad habits are often only a way of dealing with stress and patience. Since every weekend, bites to the internet shop can all be an easy answer to stress and boredom.

However, this cannot be the way. New, healthy stress management and patience methods can be learned and replaced by misconduct.

Deepening surface problems can cause stress or resistance, of course. Those problems could be hard to think about, but you should be honest about yourself if you are serious about the changes. Are certain convictions of such misconduct or reasons implied? Do you have anything worse— fear, event or conviction?

To overcome them, it is essential to recognize the causes of your bad habits.

You don't remove bad habits, you substitute them.

All of your habits— good or bad— are in your life for a reason. These behaviors will assist you somehow, even if they are bad for you otherwise.

Smoking and drugs sometimes have a biological benefit. Sometimes it is like being in a wrong relationship is emotional. And in many cases your bad habits are stress-controlled. Bite the nails, pull the hair, touch your foot or, for instance, strain the jaw.

These "benefits" or reasons also extend to lesser bad habits.

When you open the e-mail box when you start your computer, for example, you may feel connected. Your productivity is lost, your attention is shifted and your stress is overwhelmed when you look at all emails. But you don't feel like you're missing and you're still missing.

Bad habits are hard to get rid of, because they have some benefit in your life. Instead, a new practice which has the same advantage is required to replace bad habits. Simple tips such as' just stop' rarely work afterwards.

For instance, it is wrong to stop smoking when you are stressed. Instead of cigarettes, one should develop another way to cope with stress.

This means that some of your life needs are dealt with by bad habits. Therefore, it is better to replace bad habits by healthier behaviors that meet the same needs. If you only expect bad habits to break without replacing them, you won't meet certain needs. The term' Don't do' will be difficult to adhere in future.

How to break a bad habit

Here are some additional ideas for breaking your bad habits and thinking about the process in a new way.

There are several other ideas here to break your bad behavior and to reconsider the process.

Choose to change your bad habits. If you face the fear or patience that's accountable for your incorrect habits, you must respond in advance best. What do you want to do if you have the urgency to smoke?

When Facebook asks you to give up, what will you do? Whatever it is, regardless what you do, you need a plan for what you do instead of a bad habit. (For example: breathing exercises, instead.)

Cut out as many triggers as you can. Don't go to the bar if you smoke while you drink. If you're eating cookies, throw them away when they're in your house. If you first get the TV remote when you sit on the couch, then hide the remote in the cupboard, or maybe in another room. Make it easier for yourself to break bad habits by avoiding those things that often cause them.

Your environment is making your poor habits easier for you right now and making it more difficult to achieve healthy habits. You can modify the workspace and change the result.

You can join forces with someone else. How often are you trying to eat in private? Or maybe you stopped smoking, but did you keep it? (Nobody's going to see you fail like that, isn't it?)

Instead, you're supposed to combine and leave with someone. Both of you can hold each other to account and celebrate your winnings together. A strong motivator knows that someone else is expecting you to get better off.

Successfully visualize yourself. Take care to throw away cigarettes or buy a good meal or wake up early. Whatever the wrong habit, you will try to break, crush, smile, and enjoy your accomplishments. See that a new identity is being built up.

You don't have to be someone else, you just have to go back to the old one. So often, we believe that we must be a completely new person to break our poor habits. The reality is, you've already had to be someone without your bad habits. It's very unlikely, in fact, that you've had these poor practices all your life. You don't have to stop smoking, just come back as a non-smoking person. You don't have to be a good individual. Well, once again, you just need to be healthy. Even if it was years ago, you lived without that poor habit, so you're sure to be able to do it again.

One thing is simple to judge for not working better, one has to say to oneself how much you suck every moment you fall or error. You have to use "but" to solve this adverse self-talk.

Finish the phrase with "but" whenever this occurs...

- "I'm fat and out of shape, but a few months later I could be in shape."
- "I'm foolish and I'm not respected by anyone, but I'm working for a precious ability."
- "I'm a failure, but sometimes in life everybody fails."

Plan for failure. Now and then we all slip up. As a particular saying goes, "Whenever you screw up, skip a workout for a while, eat bad enough healthy foods, or sleep in, that doesn't make you a bad person. It makes you human. Welcome to the fantastic club."

Therefore, rather than beating yourself up over a specific mistake, have a plan for it. We all get off the track, what distinguishes top performers from everybody else is that they get up strongly and goes back on the track very quickly.

Taking the First Step to Breaking Bad Habits

It's simple to feel like you are feeling your poor practices. You can feel guilty or waste your time dreaming about how things are... but these ideas bring you off the truth.

Rather, this knowledge shows you how to create changes. What happens to your bad habits? Every day, how often do you do it?

Where are you? Who are you with? What triggers and causes the conduct to commence?

Tracking these problems simply helps you understand the conduct and gives you dozens of suggestions to stop it.

Here's an easy way to start: just check how often your bad practice happens every day. Put in your pocket a piece of document with a pen. Mark it on your document every moment your poor practice occurs. Take all the tally marks and calculate your sum at the start of the day.

At first it is not your objective to judge or guilty about unhealthy or unproductive behavior. The only objective is to know when and how often it occurs. Encircle the issue with a wrap of your neck. In this post, you can then begin implementing the thoughts and break your poor habits.

It requires time and energy to break poor practices, but most people have to persevere.

Many individuals who break their poor practices often attempt to die before they do it. You may not succeed immediately, but this doesn't mean you can't.

Chapter 2
The First On The First Things
First List: Spirituality

The previous chapter would seem like the whole book, but, it's just the tip of the iceberg compared to the detailed explanation of each point on our list.

Habits need three elements— the cue, the reward and the routine, according to an author Charles Duhigg. To produce any automatic reaction effectively, all the three must be nailed.

The cue is merely a matter of conditions concerning the practice. Take, for instance, the brushing of your teeth, which you (hopefully) do at least twice a day. You're most probable to do that when you wake up and go to sleep. You likely need to wash in the bathroom. You may be by yourself, too, or your wife may be there, too. You might be caused or "cued" to do it because, well, your mouth smells mucky, or you ate something with garlic. Most of us don't believe much about washing our teeth, we just do it out of practice. We don't spend hours anticipating the act, or even thinking about it. It's just going to be completed.

The reward is whatever helps activate a "muscle memory" or a Pavlovian reaction. In classical conditioning, pets (or individuals) are instructed to conduct a job and then honored with a treat. Eventually, the existence of the cue will cause a reaction. Whether it's budgetary, exercise or even dental hygiene habits, a reward is a mandatory part of the process. Good practices are producing excellent outcomes. In our dental brushing instance, the prize is a smooth mouth, a reduced dental charge, an absence of neck pain, and perhaps even the fact that you'd rather happily prevent a lesson from your dental hygienist.

Brushing of your teeth is one daily habit we've learned from a very young age which is healthy, vital, and life-changing.

The routine is a very simply one putting the cue, the act and the reward all together. Once you pool these three elements together: 1. My mouth feels mucky, 2. I brush my teeth, 3. My mouth feels better—you have the complete recipe for a good habit.

But here's the cool component, and the BIG reason for establishing healthy habits is so important: habits, once formed, use a distinct portion of our brain. We don't have to think about it, we just do it, and our mental energy isn't drained. The more healthy practices we can generate, the more efficient, the richer and the more prosperous we can become.

It's a good idea to waste time thinking about what practices you really want to create and what's most essential to you. Journaling or just writing down your healthy practices in the future can really assist. Here's a lot of excellent practices (beyond brushing) to assist you get more effective, happy and less stressed out. Try to apply some of these excellent practices to your regular lives as "beginning habits"— and it's only up there!

1. Keep things tidy

Pick up, keep stuffs organized, and even make our beds feel safer. It prepares us for tourists, enables us to be more effective, enables us to sleep better at night, and even enables us to get along better with our wife and kids.

It's likely not realistic to imagine two hours of washing every day from the roof to the ground. And every single day, vacuuming, dusting? This is not going to occur. But just going through the kitchen, gathering up products lying around, tidy up spills as they do, and rinsing your meals and placing them in the dishwasher can create a distinction. Most significant of them all? It prevents the mess from escalating, which prevents us from lashing out our wives and kids, or from being upset with ourselves.

Try setting a timer when you're just beginning to create up for that practice. Before you go to the bathroom or even before you settle down to watch a TV — whatever your daily routine — go through your house for 15 minutes. Pick up the products, placed on the beds, and wash off the surfaces. Make it a habit to rinse the dish after you've eaten it and make your bed as soon as you get up. Your day and your approach will profit.

2. Mindfullly manage your money

One of the finest habits of a highly individual? They're mindful of money management. Expenditure may be regular and automatic. When we get into the habit of cleaning a credit card every turn, it can rapidly spiral out of control and become a hazardous mess.

One of the greatest methods to get into the practice of mindful money management is to take some time off spending it all together. This may be a task, but when it's over, you'll be astounded by how much more you're talking about before you swipe your card.

Make it a practice to check your bank account and your budget every day. Just five minutes a day spent staring at it and checking that events are moving properly can cause issues straight away. Put your cash home in your purse, or position your coins in a bag every moment you invest it. Make it a practice that you stash the "additional" shift back. Wait a minute and see how quickly that adds up.

3. Choose gratitude

One practice that can alter your view almost immediately is to be willing to choose an approach of appreciation. Successful individuals are universally willing to define beneficial stuff in their lives and demonstrate gratitude for them. When I had a particularly hard moment with a loved one, a friend advised me to sit down and create a list of all that I liked about that individual. Whenever I was frustrated or upset with them, I would go back to that list. As stupid as it sounds, it really helped.

Focusing on what you're thankful for helps create gratitude for what you've got. It enables us feel holy, so that we can discover happiness in the normal times of life. When things go wrong, staying grateful enables us refocus on everything that's going right.

Make a practice of recognizing 3 stuff every day that you're very grateful for. It can be as easy as having a delicious breakfast, learning from a colleague, or sleeping in a hot sleep at night. If you concentrate on these 3 things every day and list them in your diary every evening (or on your mobile or anywhere you can readily revisit), you'll be amazed at how much you need to be pleased about.

4. Stay hydrated

Now we've all heard about the many benefits of drinking water: more energy, clearer skin, better digestion. Of course, that doesn't mean we're always going through. Why don't you make it a habit to drink a glass of water first every morning, or to drink more water during the day? It's not so much that you need to count your 8 glasses as punishment, but think of it as a great way to fuel your body.

Dehydration can make us feel hungry, tired, and sick. We're eating more, making poor choices, and tending to get unsafe drinks (like soda) when we're dehydrated. Take a bottle of water with you, and refill it when you can. Think about how amazing it is that we have access to water almost every day. There are many places in the world where water is a precious commodity— where water is brought in, stored tightly, and even fought. We are so blessed every time we have the opportunity to fill a bottle of water with clean, drinkable, fresh H2O whenever we want. Drink it now and appreciate it!

5. Plan your days

People who have been effective are planning it that way. They write down (and maintain) meetings, use a regular assignment list, and use their calendars as a guide to achieve their objectives.

For each item you want to do, find the time on your calendar and write it down. Scheduling time for stuff like practice, housekeeping, cooking and recreation can make you feel a little odd at first, but once you get used to it, it's a wonderful way to get an general perspective of your week. Scheduling helps you manage your time wisely so that you can maximize your rewards and anticipate the needs of your family.

One of the excellent habits to get into is the practice of checking over your calendar and writing your to - do list straight before you go to sleep. You can go to bed knowing that you have a scheme for the next day, and often your subconscious will work out alternatives to issues in your sleep.

6. Put your family first

Strengthening family relationships and considering the needs of your spouse and your children is one of the most important factors in any decision. In today's culture, we talk a lot about "the life you want" and success of the "Me." We also see a lot of unhappy marriages and a lot of divorce. These things are not always related, of course, but putting the needs of another person before your own really does make a difference.

I'm not saying to be a doormat or to always cave to the demands of your children, but I am saying that in every decision, make it a habit to consider, "Will this keep my children safe, happy and secure? Will this keep my spouse safe, happy and secure, and strengthen our relationship?" If you make it a habit to carefully and purposefully ask these questions first, before jumping into a decision, your entire family will benefit.

Make family time a priority and make your children a priority. Before you commit to another activity or jam another thing into an already packed schedule, be certain you're not overriding the needs of those closest to you. Every marriage needs a little one-on-one time, a date night, or some romance to keep that spark alive. Say I love you and mean it—but also make it a habit.

7. Get up early

I'm an early-riser. It's not so much that I'm a morning person, per se, but I find that if I want to achieve everything I set out to do on any given day, getting up early gives me time to get started. It gets me going before I'm faced with family needs and sets the tone and foundation for a successful day.

Set your alarm for the same time every day. Even on weekends. Want to get in the habit of getting up earlier? If you determine the best time and work back in ten-minute increments per week, you'll be getting up earlier in no time. Get to bed at a similar time each night and if you need more sleep, get to bed earlier (rather than sleeping later). Don't rob tomorrow of success to fit in another chapter tonight. Instead, put it away until later and let your body get the sleep you need.

This can be one of the most difficult habits to start, but once you do, you'll wonder why you didn't do it sooner. Early-risers are more productive and find more time to address problems at the start rather than playing catch up all day long. Even ten extra minutes in the morning can mean getting out the door on time and in an organized manner.

8. Prepare for success the night before

Similar to getting up early, getting ready before bed helps us make a jump tomorrow. Make it a habit to get your clothes out tomorrow, make sure you're ready to have lunch, and prepare whatever you need for breakfast, and put it out the night before. What takes 10 or 15 minutes before bed can take 20 or 30 minutes in the middle of morning chaos.

Make sure that the backpacks are ready to go, the keys are on the counter, and everything is in place for tomorrow's success. If you're going to make it a habit to be proactive and prepare for what lies ahead, in the morning, you're going to get some glitches off. (We all know that lost keys can totally devastate the schedule and the morning!)

9. Get moving

Successful, happy and efficient individuals have a periodic practice of going into some good motion every day. That doesn't necessarily imply a 5-mile walk (unless that's your thing, of course). Just having your meal break for 20 minutes to do a trip around the bank, riding the steps more often, or even parking your vehicle a little further away from the grocery store can really add up.

If you have a hard time making a habit move, there are a lot of applications and equipment to assist. Check out the fitness tracker, such as Fitbit or Nike+ FuelBand. A lot of fitness trackers can be laid to vibrate every hour or less to remind you to remain active. This doesn't mean you're going to have to work out every half hour or anything. Just move: going up to a glass of water or taking a fast jaunt to a copyer can bring more motion to your lives. Make a habit of movement.

10. Rest

While it's important to put your family first, this doesn't imply you should totally forgo your own requirements. Truly happy, productive individuals understand when they need to take a break and when they need to feed themselves.

This doesn't always have to be a spa day or a shopping spree. Find little presents or donations to offer yourself all day— save a cup of tea, taste it, drink it gently, and feel the heat between your fingers and the water on your skin. Think of it as a gift, really. Take the time to concentrate on it and be mindful of it.

Connect with a buddy for 10 minutes and participate in a discussion without diversion. Do exercises you like or take a stroll and explore the universe around you. Listen to a song that you enjoy, or take the moment to indulge yourself in a magazine, a hot tub, or some lengthy periods. Enjoy a piece of dark chocolate or a sweet piece of fruit. Whatever you really love, take the moment to be mindful and offer yourself something unique. Make this "me moment" a practice and do it every day. It might be difficult to discover the moment to nurture yourself, but it's essential. Do it with no guilt and appreciate it.

Do you want to be happier, healthier and more prosperous in your career? Making tiny but beneficial adjustments to your regular routine can not only reset your habits, but effectively assist your brain function more effectively and provide the much required boost you need to move in the correct direction. Don't lose out on the ten easy daily practices that might just alter your lives!

Chapter 3
Understanding The How To
Deal With Money

You can actually live off taking the moment to manage your money in a much better way. It can help you stay on top of your bills and save you more than £ 1,000 a year. You can use these additional money to pay off any debt that you may have, to pay for your pension, or to spend it on your next vehicle or holiday. Read more about money management advice, including how to set up a budget, stick to it, and how to save more money for other unforeseen expenditures.

How to set up a budget

Getting your budget back on track

Paying off loans and credit cards

Set a savings goal

If you're overwhelmed by your debts

How to set up a budget?

Account dashboard

Do you have more than one account for that? New services mean that you can now see all of your accounts in a single banking app. Find out more about it.

The first step to take in controlling your finances is by having a budget.

It's going to take a little effort, but it's a great way to get a quick snapshot of the money you've got in and out of here.

Setting up a budget means you're:

Less likely to end up in debt

Less likely to get caught out by unexpected costs

More likely to have a good credit rating

More likely to be accepted for a mortgage or loan

Able to spot areas where you can make savings

In a great position to save up for a holiday, a new car, or another treat

What you need?

Over half of the households in the United Kingdom have a regular budget. Most people say that it gives them peace of mind about how much they spend, and makes them feel better about life in general. Use our Budget Planner tool to better manage your money.

To get started on your budget, you'll need to figure out how much you're going to spend on:

Household bills

Living costs

Financial products (insurance…)

Family and friends (presents…)

Travel (car costs, public transport…)

Leisure (holidays, sport, restaurants…)

Just get as much information as you can about your income and expenditure (bills, bank statements...) and get started.

You can save your information and get back to it any time you like it.

Alternatively, you can set up a budget using a spreadsheet or write it down on paper.

There are also some great free budgeting apps available, and your bank or building company may have an online budgeting tool that takes information directly from your transactions.

Getting your budget back on track

If you invest more than you get in, you need to work out where you can cut back.

It could be as easy as having lunch at home, or canceling a gym membership that you don't use.

You can also hold an expenditure diary and maintain a note of everything you're purchasing for a month.

Or, if you spend most of your cash on a bank card, check at your bank account last month and see where your cash goes.

Get everyone involved

Get everyone involved with keeping the budget in your family.

Sit down together, make a plan that you can all stick to.

Work out how much money you're going to spend and agree on what each of you will have.

Should you manage money jointly or separately?

Cutting your household bills and your mortgage. For many of us, household bills make up a huge piece of our expenditure.

The great news is that it is very easy to save hundreds of pounds off your bills by following these tips.

You can also save hundreds and even thousands of pounds by shopping around for a new mortgage, or by looking at the one you already have.

Why it pays to review your mortgage regularly.

Be flexible

Life is unpredictable, so try to review your budget and expenditure if there is a change, or at least every couple of months.

You might get a pay increase, which means you can save more, or you might find that your household bills are increasing.

Chapter 4
The Underrated Value Of Family

Family is a significant part of our lives. It enables us to enhance our personalities. It enables us shape our lives as well. It teaches us the importance of love, affection, care, trustworthiness, and self - confidence, and offers us with the instruments and tips needed to be successful in life.

Family is a place where you can always be yourself. It's a place that accepts you for what you are. That's where you're totally free of tension and there's everyone to assist you. When you're surrounded by issues, the family supports you. It enables you to survive and bring joy and happiness to life through hard times.

Decency is very essential in everyday life communication. It enables us to establish a powerful connection with others and to make us a very soft, smart and likable individual. Everyone enjoys being in such a person's company. Family contributes to bringing decency into our lives that is essential to lead a happy life.

Building a productive and extremely rewarding profession is one of the most significant goals of our lives. Our families are helping us to build a powerful future. It provides us useful suggestions about prospects for distinct careers. Not only will it guide us in selecting the best, but it also enables us to cover educational costs financially. Therefore, it enables us to create a healthy future.

The significance of family is likely to be realized when you went on vacation or celebrate an event without family members. It was very difficult to celebrate an event or go on vacation without being surrounded by members of the family. Probably at that moment we understand how essential they are to us. We came to understand the value of our families at that moment.

Most people today don't understand the family's value. They prefer to spend with their colleagues most of their moment. But it was their family that helped them get rid of issues when they were surrounded by issues. It was our family that came to assist us at the moment when even our greatest friends refused   to assist us. It is therefore very essential to give significance to their families above all else and to love spending time with family members for every person.

The family is God's greatest and most significant blessing. It will be the first exercise in quite a while with others. Family is a significant word. It implies you have a sense of safety, you have somebody you can depend on, who you can talk about your challenges with. However, it likewise implies common regard and obligation for each other.

What family intends to me is love and somebody will consistently be there for you through the great occasions and the awful. It is tied in with empowering, getting, trust, comfort, exhortation, values, ethics, beliefs, and confidence. Every one of these things are fundamental to me in light of the fact that in my life they make me have a sense of safety and glad. This is one of the principle reasons why the family is imperative in our life. In this book, it is indispensable to stress the significance of family in our day by day life.

Utmost Protection and Security

Family is essential because it provides love, cooperation and a valuable structure to all its members. Family members are teaching each other, serving each other, and sharing the happy and sorrowful time of life. Families offer an atmosphere of personal growth. Family is the single largest effect of a child's lifetime. Children put their trust in families and relatives to protect them from their earlier phases of life and to fulfill their wishes. Parents and friends make the child's main connection. Family provides all or any member with security, identity and morals, regardless of age. Once a member of the family feels uncomfortable, he goes to the family for assistance. He learns about his self - sense and gains a life - based foundation. This basis involves family values that make up the concept of their own moral code.

It also demonstrates the significance of family following traditions and culture. Cultural convictions are experiences that families often evolve alongside each other, whether they involve holidays, holidays or even religious facilities. Not only do these experiences produce memories for years to come back, they also give family members a higher sense of happiness. Families bond with each member and make them feel essential.

First step of receiving basic values of life

A family is the primary school wherein a kid gets the fundamental estimations of life. He adapts great habits in the family. The ethics and qualities learnt in family become our directing power. They make our character. They establish the framework of our reasoning.

I feel lucky to be conceived in a family where value is instilled in early adolescence. Family is a significant and most grounded unit of society. It holds incredible significance in public activity. A general public is comprised of families. Our family has been known for order and qualities. We give incredible significance to qualities and ethics throughout everyday life. Since our initial youth we are instructed to regard the older folks and love the youngsters. We took in the exercise of reliability and genuineness from our granddad. It is because of the great instruction of our grandparents that we could exceed expectations both in games and training. Since our youth we have been placed into the propensity for rising promptly in the first part of the day. This naturally affects our wellbeing and physical wellness.

Settling on a correct decision in picking the correct life accomplice family value impacts each stroll of our life. The opportunity has already come and gone that family value be ensured and be treated as an apparatus to wipe out debasement, appetite, imbalance, and wrongdoing and disdain in our general public.

To shape a child's future

The family is your blood and they are the individuals who acknowledge you for what your identity is, who might effectively observe you grin and who adore you regardless. The family is one and only spot where your life starts and love never end. You may have bunches of individuals throughout your life, however you won't locate a solitary individual who cares the most precisely same as your parent. Some of you may not concur with me, yet this is reality that one day you will understand this by your own. A family is the main spot where kids study much after school. In school, educators show kids the subjects which will assist them with finding a great job in future. Be that as it may, in the home, Family shows kid's propensities, discipline which help them to get a new line of work as well as assistance them to carry on with an ideal life in future. So the family is significant for children. At the point when infants turn out from mother's belly, they see their parent first and from there on they invested the majority of the energy with their family until go to class. During that 3 or 4 years is extremely significant for infants to become more acquainted with some essential propensities from guardians, sisters or siblings. So on that period, they become acquainted with numerous things from family. None of you going to show unfortunate propensities for your infant, I accept. Guardians must be cautious in activities before their infants in light of the fact that your child takes in propensities and control from you as it were.

This is one of the fundamental reasons why the family is significant in our life. This is one of the extraordinary focus points of family and none of us ever understand this whenever. You may have heaps of companions or relations or office mates. They will be with you in your cheerful occasions or any fruitful accomplishments. Be that as it may, your parent or sisters or siblings are the main ones will remain with you in your hard and troublesome occasions. Your parent is the one in particular who comprehends you significantly more than some other individuals do on the planet. Since they are your makers and they are the main one's going with you from the earliest starting point. So they comprehend your emotions and consistently there for you at whatever point you need somebody bounteously. This is the intensity of family. There are numerous individuals can support you, however the family will help you at whatever point you are distant from everyone else.

Helps building an ideal society

A perfect family is an extraordinary case of the entire society. Father, Mother, children every one of them need to work so as to construct a perfect family. In the event that any of them fizzled, at that point the entire family fallen. This happens especially these days. The great name of the entire family destroyed by a solitary individual from the family. That is extremely tragic yet nothing to accomplish for that. In any case, on the off chance that each relative buckles down and fabricates a perfect family, at that point they are a genuine case of that entire society. Family impacts particularly in the public arena and society impacts especially in the nation. So a perfect nation works by the legislature as well as every single relative. So every family is the chief key to the general public. This is the reason the family is significant in our life.

Family esteems are a lot of unwritten decides and codes that makes and helps manufacture our recognition, vision towards society and numerous things that we face in our everyday life. Solid family esteems can impart more noteworthy clearness in basic leadership with respect to our life and prompts a generally simpler and increasingly healthy lifestyle. Giving solid qualities as a parent secures a youngster as well as make a humanized cognizant native and help move society towards an increasingly innocuous tomorrow. Solid family esteems can help check all the good and moral debasement in different backgrounds which generally at last adds to disparity neediness wrongdoing and so forth.

In the present immovable world, the best individual are the individuals who can take snappy choices about what they need from life. Family esteem that causes you recognize what is ethically right and what suits your worth framework. Today the single biggest errand in hands of guardians is shielding their youngsters from outside impact which are significantly negative in nature. Infusing solid family esteems in kid since adolescence is one such measure that can guarantee their security in when direct supervision of kid has turned out to be close to unimaginable…

Chapter 5
The Misunderstood Meaning Of:
Self Love

In the event that you had ask me whether I adored myself, I'd say yes. I love myself, I however I'm very quiet, brilliant and interesting.

But, when I lied in my bed in a serious depression constantly tormenting myself with considerations like "I'm bad "," I don't worth it "or" I don't love myself "- I understood that I was a long way from genuinely adoring myself.

So what does" self-love "is? It took me a couple of months to completely get it.

Self-love is one of these ideas that you simply get. You don't logically get it. You feel it.

F or my situation I read about it, I rehearsed what was proposed in books and articles, and after that one day I just got it. My outlook moved. What's more, I began adoring myself. Much the s a me as this.

How to get to that point?

Learn. Peruse. Find. Continue searching, and one day you will simply get it. It's exactly like yoga. You practice for quite a while attempting to get into that one posture. It appears to be extremely intense. And after that one day you do. What's more, you understand how simple it is once you get it. You're in impeccable equalization. but, from that minute, you recollect how to do this posture. Every so often you may lose your parity, however you comprehend what it feels like to be in the posture – and you can return.

Same goes for self-love

What isn't self-love

Numerous individuals (as I used to) think they love themselves, yet what we feel is somewhat the liking of self.

When you figure out how to lose a couple of kilos, when you do your hair and makeup and look extraordinary – you such as yourself.

When you accomplish something important – you like yourself.

When you assist someone else – you like yourself.

In any case, what when the opposite occurs?

In the event that you put on a couple of kilos, okay still look in the mirror with the adoration and appreciation? Do you like yourself notwithstanding when your hair is muddled and you got a couple of pimples all over?

Or then again what when you acted truly mean to someone – do despite everything you such as yourself at that point?

What we regularly take for self-love is a contingent enjoying of the individual we are.

Rather than unadulterated love, we judge ourselves. On the off chance that you we accomplish something right, we remunerate ourselves with love. In any case, when we accomplish something awful, we rebuff ourselves by removing that affection. We become the harshest punisher in our lives.

So what is true self-love?

True love in an unqualified sense of love, gratitude, and recognition of oneself. What does it imply unconditionally? No matter what you do, you're always in love with the same strength.

Now I understand it might make sense when you read it, but you might be asking, how are you going to get to that stage? How can you get it?

I found the following steps to be helpful in the journey towards self-love:

1. Become aware of your inner voice

The first thing you need to do is to know how to handle yourself. We all speak to ourselves in our minds, but we are not always fully aware of that tone.

So, first phase—be aware of your internal voice. Pay attention to what it says.

Notice what you're most likely to say yourself. What do you say when you do something wonderful, and what do you say when you fail?

Here are a few circumstances in which you should be aware of your internal voice:

When you wake up and look in the mirror

When you get scolded by your boss

When somebody is mean to you

When you are mean to someone

When you act on your anger

When you see someone in need, but you maintain wandering without assisting them.

When you put on weight

When you make a mistake at work

When you eat some unhealthy food

When you skip your work-out session

When you lie to somebody

When you make someone cry

When you feel lazy

When you rest
In all these moments, are you still loving and caring for yourself?

If not – go to Step 2.

2. Take control of your inner voice

The things you've heard in your head have been there all your lives. Maybe you haven't given attention to it before–in which event you might be surprised to know some of the stuff you say to yourself.

But the reality is, you've been carrying these posts to yourself for years. And the more we hear, the more we think in it. Which implies that all the adverse things you say to yourself have become your strong convictions.

But you can change them. But Step by step.

Now that you're conscious of your inner voice, next moment you find yourself stating something bad to yourself, pause and say, "Cancel, cancel." Little trick, but it effectively gives a signal to your subconscious mind to overlook what you were just thinking.

After canceling, tell a fresh thing to yourself –this time a helpful, loving and caring signal. And just continue doing this.

I understand it will seem like a lie at first. You're not going to think in that fresh beautiful message. That's okay. Keep doing it, and over moment, you're going to be friendly to the signal, and lastly, you're going to trust it.

3. Treat yourself just like a child

People often wonder how they should speak to themselves. After being so tough on us, we don't understand what that fresh voice should be like.

So, to assist you modify the sound of your inner voice, just consider yourself as a kid. Some individuals call this your inner child. Tuning your inner child enables you to look at yourself without judgment.

You see yourself as this little, fragile animal that just wishes to be loved.

The time you see yourself as a kid, you will realize that the severe judgment is melting away. It's just that easy!

We all have internal kids in us, after all. There are needs that have never been encountered when we were very young, and we bring these requirements into our adult life. We may be suppressing them, pushing them into the subconscious, and not even realizing that they are there, but I ensure that they are there.

Treating yourself as a kid enables you to meet those requirements.

4. Love yourself emotionally and physically

This is my favourite part of the whole process.

What are you going to do when you love someone? Think of your relatives, your brothers, your girlfriend or your greatest friend. Do you get presents from them? Do you have to bring them out on a date? Are you paying for them? Do you spend quality time together, huh?

Love is a sensation, love is a verb. Love is just as much about feeling as it's about doing!
So now is the moment to do something of your own love.

Think of all the stuff you're enjoying that give you joy. And just do it with yourself.

If you've never attempted it before the concept of doing something on your own could scare you a little–I understand that's how I feels.

At the moment, my healer proposed that I take myself out on a date once a week. And she proposed that you go to a good lunch.

Dinner alone, huh? I feels like the greatest loser sitting alone at the table!

But you know what, if you do, it's a clear sign that you don't enjoy yourself yet. Because once you do, you're going to begin enjoying yourself spending time.

And this is the whole point of the workout. It's to be a friend of yours and feel totally pleased and complete even when there's no one else next to you.

We need to avoid depriving ourselves of the stuff we love and create us comfortable.

From now on, grant yourself approval to do the stuff you love doing. You don't always need to do stuff that create sense or create your profession. Spending time to do stuff just because you like them is just as essential.

Here are some few ideas that will help you on how to get started with "doing" self-love:

Take yourself out for a very nice dinner

Paint (or do any other type of art that you enjoy most and that allows you to express creatively)

Write (you can write poems, a book, or a keep a daily journal)

Take photographs

Visit museum

Cook something healthy

Drink a green smoothie

Read your favourite book (and yes, it can be that love story you love)

Watch a romantic comedy

Buy yourself a nice dress

Get a manicure

Go to SPA (massages are my favourite things for self-love!)

Go for a yoga class

Dance (and you can perfectly go crazy in your house)

Listen to your favourite music

Play with animals

Stay in nature

Go for a walk

Do nothing (yep – just sit, or lie down and do absolutely nothing)

The more you exercise self-love, the greater the signal you transmit to yourself: "You deserve it." It's an important, enjoyable way to exercise self-love.

So just begin right now. Follow all of these 4 measures. And understand that if you do it, you'll just get it one day. You're going to wake up and think distinct. You're going to be in love. It's with yourself.

Love,

What Self-Love Means: Follow these 20+ Ways to Be Good to Yourself

"Self-love requires you to be honest about your current choices and thought patterns and undertake new practices that reflect self-worth." ~Caroline Kirk

If one more person told me to go love myself I was going to levitate into the air and pull one of those impossible martial arts moves from Crouching Tiger, Hidden Dragon. I was sick of it!

What does it imply to love me? Were they speaking about bubble baths, pedicures, and rubber masks? It turns out that there is so much more to self-love than just to spoil ourselves. This is the hard way I discovered out.

About a year and a half earlier, after a poor breakup, I nearly killed. I had spent so much of my energy making the relationship job that I had totally ignored my own requirements and taken away my authority and accountability for happiness.

As I wrote about this, when I lastly acquired the bravery to put an end to an addictive and painful partnership, I had to live with the consequences of absence of self-love.

I have tried to consume, sleep, or keep my regular working going. I devoted every hour of my waking up to myself, attempting to comprehend how and why I got there. I had to know, because whatever it was, if I didn't participate, it was going to be the end of the path for me. Well, I realized it.

I produced mixed media collages, diaryed, watched The Notebook five more times, yelled, and called friends to maintain me company while I ate my few meals every day.

Throughout this time, I've found places in my story where I haven't been present to my existence, my body or my soul. I've just been there. I discovered the areas where I had left myself and then got angry at the other individual for not meeting my requirements.

The truth of the matter was, I didn't have a large enough internal container to keep the love I wanted so much, even if I got it, because my self-love tank had shrunk down to the size of a bottle cap.

Finally, it became very clear to me that there was one main reason I had gotten there: I didn't understand anything about self-love.

This realization has led me to an unceasing quest for the significance of self-love, internally and sexually.

I have discovered that self-love is not a target; it is a habit. Self-love is the basis upon which we construct a happy life. Without self-love, we have nowhere to bring in the esteem or abundance that comes to us.

You don't know what it sounds like to enjoy yourself? Here's exactly what I've discovered. Self-love is the...

1. Choosing oneself, even if it implies upsetting others and no longer being common. Even if it implies we're leaving a group before anyone else because we feel exhausted, bored, or simply feel like we're finished to the audience.
2. Telling what is true of us, not swallowing phrases that convey what we really feel, believe, or want to do.
3. To give our body the nourishment, rest, exercise, and comfort it needs to the best of our ability.
4. Wearing dresses that create us feel nice and suit our character instead of wearing clothes that are fashion that we use to impress others.
5. Building a life that we enjoy while we are single, instead of waiting for our princess to show up to discover life and be pleased.
6. Accepting ourselves with the good, the bad, the hideous, the sexy, and the fragrant— all of it— and appreciating ourselves as a whole.
7. Making time to do whatever we love, to just play, without worrying about wasting time.
8. Owning our internal and exterior beauty and complimenting ourselves without feeling guilty, stupid, or self-righteous.

9. Not rehashing our past mistakes and dragging ourselves into a dark place when we know that we can only learn from the past; we can't alter it.

10. Spending some value, connecting time with ourselves instead of always watching TV or spending time on the Internet.

11. Use choice to share our soul, ego, and dreams with others.

12. Trusting the road our soul is on and making a real attempt to become adeliberate co-creator of our destiny.

13. Not to blame our relatives for our present problems, and to look for ways to cure our injuries and alter our dysfunctional patterns of behavior by reaching out to ministers, therapists, trainers, and healers.

14. Follow what our gut/intuition tells instead of living out of our brains and egos.

15. Staying in our integrity, both when it gets to ourselves and when it comes to communicating with others outside the globe. This involves maintaining an eye on models such as lying, manipulation, co-dependent, withholding, and feigning.

16. Allowing ourselves to dream large, without contaminating those dreams with decisions, our perceived constraints, or the absence of a sense of merit.

17. Knowing how we spend our emotional, mental, economic, and physical power, and whether these actions take pleasure, relationship, nurturing, remainder and creativity back to our life.

18. Take accountability for all of our experience. Knowing that we are capable of greater self-awareness and access to our intuition when it comes to creating life decisions.

19. Not to label ourselves with the opinions of others, but to have the courage to look inside to see if there might be any truth to them.
20. Learn to set limits that safeguard and nurture our interactions, with ourselves and others.
21. Allowing us to make errors and not berating ourselves for creating them. Instead, we choose to appreciate our desire to learn and grow.
22. Refusal to seek permission or consent to be on our own. Recognizing that we, like all the others, deserve to take up room on this planet just as we are right now.

And finally, self-love is:

23. Loving and recognizing ourselves even if we have failed miserably to achieve some of these self-love objectives.

No one else can give us this stuff. No one else can bring our vitamins for us or stop us from committing a self-loathing assault.

Even if we land the best partner on the planet, this person won't be allowed to make us happy and feel valued unless we create room for him inside by exercising self-love. This is why self-love is a task on the inside.

From my heart to your heart…

Chapter 6
Mastering Our Own Soul
Through: Exercise

Most of you understand that practice is nice for you. What most people don't understand is how good it is. And the reasons are not what you might think about it. Sure, the esthetic benefits are important, as is the impact on your health and well-being.

But integrating regular exercise into your life can have a much deeper impact.

As a huge believer in the positive effects that regular exercise can have on a person's life and here are 10 ways that can make you believe that regular exercise can make you a better person:

1. It improves your self-esteem.

Think about the last moment you were looking in the mirror with your clothes off. Have you been pleased? Disgusted? Disgusted? Apathetic, huh? Being fit or operating towards fitness can play a enormous part in how you feel about yourself. Being pleased with who you are as a individual is far deeper than what you look like.

2. It motivates and inspires you to do more and be more.

When you have a consistent habit of exercising, it changes the way you see the world. All of a sudden, those obstacles that you once saw as insurmountable are impossible to overcome.

3. It builds confidence.

Trust is one of those items that can have a important effect on many fields of your lives. Walking around with your head held low and uncertain of yourself is the quickest way to get mediocrity. In my knowledge, the best way to build trust is to look and feel like a million dollars. When you're fit and safe, you become a more vibrant and lively version of yourself. It's going to carry you over to everything you do and who you are.

4. It inspires others to improve themselves.

You may not even think about it, but when people, especially those close to you, see you working on yourself, they can become inspired to change themselves.

5. It teaches your children the importance of hard work.

Do you want your kids to believe it's OK to lie down on the couch eating Dorito's and watching Starsky and Hutch's reruns? Show them how important it is to be successful. Teach them the significance of eating high-quality food, and why they should play sports, run, and burn calories.

6. It teaches you discipline.

As Jim Rohn said, "discipline is the distinction between goal and achievement." If there's one region that I see time and again that individuals are struggling with, it's getting the discipline to regulate their unhealthful practices. It's extremely difficult for many individuals to be prepared to choose a piece of fruit over a doughnut.

But once regular exercise is part of your life, those choices become easier, because subconsciously (or consciously) you don't want to destroy your attempts by creating unsanitary choices.

7. It can make you happier.

And after all, we all want to live a happy life, don't we? Regular workout will kick those endorphins into elevated shoes and energize you for the day. It also produces chemical dopamine, which creates a feeling of happiness and enjoyment.

8. It can improve your relationships.

Over the last 25 years, I've gone through many different periods of activity and inactivity. One thing I've found is that when I am working out on a regular basis, my relationships seem to be deeper and more meaningful. Why? It's because we feel great about ourselves and tend to reflect how we feel about ourselves onto our partners.

9. It changes your attitude.

Attitude is all about it. Everything that occurs in our life is nothing more than an event. It's all about how we choose to respond to occurrences that make a distinction. This is where the approach is so crucial. Seeing something as favorable can totally change the result.

10. It allows you to challenge yourself to be better every day.

Personal growth is something most individuals are striving for every day. Getting out of your comfort zone, pressing your boundaries, and evaluating your physical abilities are all activities that can assist you become a better individual, both physically and mentally.

Closing Thoughts

Life is just too short for you not not to live the best of your life. Do yourself a very huge favor and start exercising on a regular basis. I know that you're going to look better, feel better, be happier, and ultimately be a better person. Just give it a notch today and see what becomes of your life.

Chapter 7
The Selfless Act Of: Giving Back

The importance of offering to others can not be understated, and that's because the key to living is giving. If you really believe about it, what's life all about? Creation of significance. How are you creating significance in your lives? It's not about what you do for yourself: it's about how you can improve the lives of the people around you–your loved ones, the people in your community, or the lives of people somewhere else in the world.

Meaning never comes from what you get, it comes from what you give. So, how can you start realizing the significance of giving?

Find Your Purpose

What is it that drives you in your lives? Are you encouraged to make a lot of cash at work? Do you appreciate being acknowledged for your achievements? Well, that's a nice beginning, but believe deeper. Why are you enjoying making cash? Is it so that you can take care of your family and feel safe? You may be pleased to be acknowledged for your accomplishments, because it helps you feel like you're getting the most of your moment, or you appreciate giving back to your sector in some manner. There is always a higher objective that drives your activities.

Now, what if you could operate towards your goal by contributing to others? This is going to assist you achieve a higher feeling of satisfaction. You may feel like you are making a significant distinction for a good cause and, eventually, getting nearer to attaining your private objectives.

Start Small And Start Today

Why don't you give back already? Is that because you feel like you don't have the time or cash to do that? It's not an absence of funds, it's a lack of resourcefulness.

A lot of individuals are waiting to offer back, but the reality is, no matter what funds you have, you can begin today. And the truth is, even if you have a very small amount of money, if you don't give back now, you won't have to be extremely effective. Contribution is a way of thinking that allows us to spend a portion of our life to assisting others–it's not about how much you have. Whether you earn $30,000 a year and spend your time to volunteer at a local community center or create $1 million a year and give a part of each paycheck, there are methods you can begin supporting others today.

Create A Ripple Effect

Think of a few individuals that you admire. Bill Gates, Oprah Winfrey, J.K. Rowling, Marc Benioff and Serena Williams are all names that come to mind. What do these individuals do on a regular basis? They are working diligently to transmit their message, to generate importance in the life of others, and to offer back. Now, believe about the beneficial effect that these individuals have had on the globe. Bill Gates, through the Bill and Melinda Gates Foundation, donated more than $30 billion to the charity.

Do you believe this kind of action is inspirational? Most people don't have the means Bill Gates has, but that doesn't mean that your contributions, too, can't encourage others. Once you begin giving back to your society, you'll see how your beneficial activities are encouraging others to get engaged. Your coworkers might want to come along to clean up your next beach, or your daughter's willing to volunteer with you at a local homeless shelter. The same goes to economic donations. If you discover a non-profit that inspires your curiosity, your colleagues and coworkers may be similarly motivated to offer as well. Create a beneficial ripple effect through your attitude.

The significance of providing to others should not be neglected. Not only will your activities profit those who reach the end of your excellent acts, but you will discover a private feeling of happiness and satisfaction through your donations. Once you create the practice of providing back on a periodic basis, even if you create a tiny donation, you will start to feel more natural and easier to do so. Start adding to the globe around you today, and be prepared to reap the advantages of offering back.

Here's a significant lesson in life: no matter how difficult you believe your life is, there's always someone who has to face difficulties that are even tougher than yours.

And it's going in a bunch of instructions. Not only fundamental items like creating cash, getting meals or having a position to sleep at night, but also the chance of engaging in some entrepreneurial initiatives or having a healthy education.

These situations are far less difficult for most individuals in the US, Europe, East Asia, and so on. With the internet at hand, we can take role in almost any venture imaginable, put together a squad of individuals from distinct jobs and skills, and begin instantly.

We can have Starbucks coffee or steak at the closest steakhouse, and so on. But what would you do without electricity or a location to purchase garments, not to mention a laptop with internet access?

Giving back is among the most important and valuable things an entrepreneur can do. Period.

And I'm not speaking about giving back in terms of "providing an inexpensive item," or "doing something for free in return for advertising space." It's just company.

Giving back is where you're giving back, and then nothing occurs. No advantages to you, no recognition, nothing concrete sends your way. Your greatest and only prize is the knowledge that you have created an important shift in someone's lives. And if not "substantial," there is still a beneficial shift.

Different cultures around the globe emphasize handing back. I grew up learning the word "seva" from my relatives and grandparents. Seva in Indian culture implies selfless service. It implies doing good for others and not expecting anything back. In a larger image, this blends into the notion of "Karm" which implies excellent actions to help others contribute to a dignified, meaningful and happy lives.

The significance of Seva has been emphasized to me in the household and guided by instance. My relatives residing in rural

India did not have a lot of money. This wasn't stopping them from doing good to others. My grandad used to pick up his rusty ancient bike and ride along unpaved highways between the fields to go to tiny farmers ' homes in the bad areas to assist them. My childhood memories consist of opening the large gate of his lovely hand-painted large concrete building with a large colourful veranda where villagers used to arrive for refuge and help. There was a joy and a musical laugh in the air that came from being good to one another that was difficult to define in words.

My father persisted with the tradition of seva. Every Tuesday, we used to go to medical clinics and give nutrition and goods to individuals suffering from leprosy, polio or other disabilities. I've been looking forward to Tuesdays. Seeing individuals smile on account of what I did led to a profound feeling of satisfaction.

Why is Giving Back important?

It opens our minds and hearts to humanity, and a greater goal is to make this universe a stronger place. It's simple to get stuck in our troubles, errors, disappointments, issues, deadlines, societal stresses, the notoriety of social media, comparisons with others, and pain from physical or mental illness.

Thinking and genuinely doing good for others has always helped me to focus on a greater intent and a greater significance in life. Gandhi said, "The best way to discover yourself is to leave yourself at the expense of others." We are all linked as human beings, and alleviating the pain of others is a privilege. Finally, it is our decision to create this earth a stronger place for our kids and future generations.

It's intriguing how handing back impacts our brains. Scientifically speaking research, including those released by Tristen Inagaki, Ph.D., from the University of Pittsburgh and Naomi Eisenberger, Ph.D., University of California, Los Angeles (UCLA) in February 2016 in Psychosomatic Medicine, have shown that granting can boost parts of the brain to a functional MRI that can decrease stress and activate a part of the brain that acts as a reward.

How To Give Back?

These are some practical ways which you might find useful in your journey of giving back:

1. Find a cause that you're enthusiastic about. They can be human rights, animal welfare, safety, migrants, schooling or something else.
2. Volunteer: Find a non-profit that works in a region you're enthusiastic about. You can attempt a website like a volunteer game or an idealist or various others. You can discover distant internet volunteering possibilities or on-site possibilities based on your accessibility of moment.
3. Donate: It could also be a few bucks or more. More than the quantity, the purpose is to make a contribution and to be a component of a bigger task. You can also choose Amazon's smile charity to contribute to Amazon when you shop online. You can choose to contribute when you shop in a grocery store. You can also choose to donate child shower or products that you

no longer make use of that can be of benefit to a project to introduce smiles to moms and children in emerging nations. So, activities like birthdays can also be given for a good cause. This is particularly helpful for children in teaching them the principles of instance and nurturing to give back to the society.

4. Advise: Generally, non-profits are looking for Advisors who will act as a guiding light in distinct parts of their activities. By being part of their consultative panel, you can use your expertise and abilities to provide advice on a specific aspect of your activities.

5. Lead: Start a chapter of a nonprofit and lead to make a difference in your local community and impact people positively.

6. Raising awareness on social media: promote the causes and organisations that you are enthusiastic about on social media. Raising awareness of these triggers can lead to activities that can create a difference in the life of others.

7. Take an instance: follow your dreams and create decisions that assist others. It's essential, in tiny or large respects, whatever you do, and you matter. There's no one like you, and there's something you need to create life easier for others.

Your little acts of kindness can make a difference in someone's life. As Confucius said, "Wherever you go, go with all your core." Whatever your interests are for the causes that you think in, you can create a distinction. The universe of selfless giving is full of joy and important times to cherish for a lifetime. I wish you luck on your private trips bringing smiles to the life of others.

Chapter 8
Mastering The Body And Soul
Through: Relaxation

Relaxation is a significant component of preserving health and well-being and being prepared to cope calmly with the stress of life. It increases your mental health and provides your body a opportunity to take a break, release muscle tension (which you may not even be conscious of), decrease blood pressure, enhance digestion (the body shifts its focus back to digestion and other maintenance and repair procedures instead of being in alert / alarm stage. Massage, practice, meditation, Tai Chi, learning books, crafts, guided imaging and yoga, etc.

The nervous system is also provided with the chance to relax during relaxation activities. A straightforward method is the following. Sit in a cozy seat or on the ground in a cozy situation. Next, tell yourself that you're going to relax totally. Start with your scalp and operate, bit by bit, down to your fingers. As you think, every portion of your body is totally soothing. Stay in a relaxed state for a few minutes. You're going to be amazed at how comfortable you can make yourself feel. Having performed this a few occasions, you will be able to differentiate between relaxed and tense states. Try to incorporate it as part of your regular routine. Being willing to feel when you're getting tense is a very helpful ability, providing you with a chance to prevent unproductive stress responses sooner, preventing headaches, muscle aches and other side-effects of elevated stress. If you discover it hard to remove stress and stress from your mind, attempt to say the phrases ' relax' or' sleep' or even' relax and sleep' over and over to stop other ideas from reaching your mind.

Another technique is to focus on the emotions and emotions you have. Other techniques may concentrate your attention on a specific portion of the body, such as the navel, or on an important item or individual. Other relaxation techniques include slow, deep breathing. You can attempt to sing a mantra at the same moment. In India, the most famous is the om, which relates to God. The concept is to take a deep breath and then, at the same moment, exhale and utter om. This is reiterated for a few minutes and is compared to an inner massage.

The ultimate technique is differential relaxation. A easy method in which you learn to relieve distinct muscles while others are being used. By evaluating which muscles you can relieve during day-to-day operations, such as traveling, you can decrease your stress and anxiety rates, leaving you with a lot more energy at the end of the day.

Breathing Exercises for Relaxation

Breathing is believed to be one of the most very efficient stress-reduction methods as it impacts the tension in your muscles, oxygenates your body, and influences emotions and ideas.

For breathing exercises to be effective, a person must –

Find the right place, away from distractions, where they can sleep comfortably.

The body must be placed in such a way that it is safe from any types, especially in the back and throat.

The individual needs to breathe slowly and deeply. Deep breathing implies that the air has to be brought down to the abdomen.

Air should be brought in through the nose and pushed out through the mouth.

Breathe gently to the count of five, then exhale to the count of six.

Continue for two or more minutes.

You may find it useful to consider what changes you feel in your body after doing this or to ask the person you are helping to consider how they feel afterwards.

Humour and Stress Relief

Research has shown that laughter can bring health benefits from reducing food cravings, increasing our pain threshold, strengthening the immune system, healing and reducing stress. Why is laughter reducing stress?

Physical Release–Raughter, like crying, can lead to emotional and physical release. Sometimes, at the same time, we can cry and laugh–"cry with laughter." This helps to release emotions.

Hormones–laughter can help reduce stress hormones such as epinephrine / adrenaline and cortisol, dopamine and growth hormones. It may increase the levels of positive hormones such as endorphins. Laughter may increase the antibody-producing cells that may increase the effectiveness of T-cells that improve our immune system.

Distraction–laugh at us to get away from our stress, anger, and negative emotions.

Internal workout — Laughter uses our diaphragm, abdominal muscles, shoulders, and leads to relaxed muscles.

Social benefits–laughter can help us interact with others, reduce stress, reduce stress, and improve interactions with others.

Perspective–sometimes people see things as a threat or a challenge. Humor can make us see things differently–in a humorous way, making things more positive and less threatening.

Using laughter to reduce stress–We can reduce stress through laughter in a variety of ways. They may include–

Watching funny films and TV programmes.

Laughing with friends and family.

Fake it up! Studies have shown that even a fake smile or laughter can have positive effects, so the more we smile, the more positive we feel.

Try as much as you could to have more fun in your life.

Try to see more humour in your life.

Relaxation techniques: Try these steps to reduce stress

Relaxation techniques can help in reducing stress symptoms and help you to enjoy a better quality of life, most especially when you have a certain disease that's holding you down. Explore relaxation techniques that can be done by yourself.

Relaxation is an excellent way to manage your stress. Relaxation is not only a matter of peace of mind or entertainment. The restfulness of your mind and body is a process that reduces stress. Relaxation techniques can assist you in tackling daily stress and stress in connection with different health conditions such as heart disease and pain.

Whether you're under stress or already under stress, you can take advantage of relaxation techniques to learn. Basic relaxation techniques can be learned easily. Relaxation techniques are often free or inexpensive, present little risk and can be practiced nearly anywhere.

Explore these simple techniques of relaxation and start to de-stress your life.

The benefits of relaxation techniques

Relaxation techniques may not be a priority in your life when you face several tasks and requirements of disease. But that means you might miss relaxation's health benefits.

Practicing relaxation techniques can have many benefits in your life, including:

Reducing muscle tension and chronic pain

Slowing heart rate

Slowing your breathing rate

Improving digestion

Maintaining normal blood sugar levels

Increasing blood flow to major muscles

Improving concentration and mood

Improving sleep quality

Reducing activity of stress hormones

Lowering fatigue

Reducing anger and frustration

Lowering blood pressure

Boosting confidence to handle problems

Use relaxation methods and other techniques of coping with positive thinking, humor, problem-solving, time management, workouts, sleeping and contacting family and friends to maximize the benefits.

Types of relaxation techniques

Health care professionals such as health practitioners complementary, physicians and psychotherapists can teach various techniques of relaxation. But you can also learn some relaxation techniques on your own if you prefer.

Relaxation techniques generally involve focusing your attention on something that calms and makes your body more aware. Which kind of relaxation you choose does not matter. What's important is that you try to relax regularly to benefit from it.

Types of relaxation techniques include:

Self-genic relief. Self-genic means something from inside you. You use both visual imaging and physical awareness to reduce stress in this relaxation technique.

You repeat words or ideas that can help you relax and reduce tension in your mind. For instance, you can imagine a peaceful atmosphere and focus on a controlled, relaxed breathing, slowering the rhythm of your heart or feeling different feelings, like relaxing one arm or leg.

The muscles are gradually relaxed. You focus on slow tightening and then relaxing each muscle group in this relaxation technique.

You can focus on how muscle strain and relaxation differ. This can help you. Your physical feelings can become more aware.

One way of relaxing your muscle progressively is to tense and relax your dogs, and work your way up to your neck and head gradually. You can also begin working with your head and neck. Strong your muscles for about 5 seconds, then relax, and repeat for about 30 seconds.

Visualization. In this relaxation technique, you can create mental pictures in a peaceful, calming place or situation.

Try to incorporate as many senses as possible to relax with visualization, including smell, sight, sound and touch. Think, for example, of the smell of salt water, the sound of crashing waves and the warmth of the sun in your body when you think about relaxing in the ocean.

Maybe you would like to close your eyes, sit still, loosen tight clothes, and focus on the breathing. Concentrate on the present and consider positive ideas.

Other relaxation techniques may include:

Deep breathing

Massage

Meditation

Tai chi

Yoga

Biofeedback

Music and art therapy

Aromatherapy

Hydrotherapy

Relaxation techniques take practice

You may become more aware of muscle strain and other physical stress feelings by learning relaxation techniques. Once you know what the stress response feels, you can consciously apply the relaxation method when you begin to feel the symptoms of stress. This can help prevent uncontrolled spiraling.

Remember, relaxation methods are skills. As with any other skills, your ability to relax develops through practice. You've got to be patient with yourself. Don't let your effort to practice relaxation methods become another form of stress on you.

If one relaxation method is not working for you, you can try another method out of the several available methods within your reach. Or rather, you can just have to see your about other options if none of your efforts at stress reduction seems to work for you.

Chapter 9
Controlling What Controls People: Fear

ear of failure, fear of refusal, fear of not being enough—fear is the common trend of life as a whole. Fear can keep us locked up in prison in a comfortable, predictable way that we can't achieve our true potential if we allow it to happen.

However, there's also a way that anxiety can serve a valuable function, helping us break through frustration to accomplish the life we really want to live. That is correct -- if you let it, fear can turn into your ultimate motivator.

In your head, if you have no choice rather than to triumph — if the only thing that matters to you is achieving your targeted goal— then nothing else matters. Sacrifices are not even going to be a question. Excuse your head from the window. You're going to do whatever is necessary to make it happen. Let your end be the justification of your means. Period.

This is how a number of the greatest people in their lives are able to overcome fear. They understand that the cost is the anxiety, unless they give every ounce of strength and focus to their goals and dreams. In contrast to allowing fear to crack and suck the fantasy's life. You know that you're really afraid that a life you need is compromise or resolved.

How can you take this view and perspective? How do you surrender to live? Fearful lifestyle and enter your true happiness?

Here are five tips to stop fear controlling your happiness and how to overcome fear:

1. Determine if your goal is a "must"

Ask yourself exactly what it will cost you if you do not decide to work on anxiety overcome. This can help you discover whether it is a' must' rather than a' should' to achieve one particular objective.

Sound unclear? Think of yourself when you turn 80 and come close to the end of your life. Look back in your own lives, now, as if you hadn't achieved your goal in your lives now. How did that affect the length of your everyday life? What are your misgivings? How much more time would you like? What would you want you to try? Can the pain and sorrow be there? You can use anxiety motivation to pursue your ultimate goal.

2. Recognize the excuses

You can easily disregard our hopes, wishes and dreams. We apologize: I don't have the money or resources, I have a family, I'm just too busy. I don't have the time enough. And behind these excuses, we begin to hide. Because they comfort. Because they comfort. They are safe. They are safe. But apologies will also take you back to where you began. So remember, the next time you get an excuse. Do you really want to be in life where you want to be? Or do you reject fear and choose to comfortably face a challenge instead? When you become more aware of the inclination of your brain to use excuses so that you are not held to account, the better you are to dismiss them.

3. Adopt a growth mindset

People often give up because they think it is beyond their ability to achieve their goal. You never learn to overcome fear and settle down and think that your goal is just not achievable, so you shouldn't try anything. But the best people are promoting a spirit of growth. You don't see your capacity as fixed, but as flexible. And they try harder in the face of a setback. A new strategy is being adopted. You are continuously looking for a solution. When things get challenging, they don't give up. Rather, they find new ways to adapt to their objectives and to work harder.

4. Pain brings valuable insight

No one in the world is successful and has no major obstacles to be overcome. The most painful experiences can help to sharpen your desires and your desires in life. Failure, deception, dead ends–all of which can be used to ponder and say, "It didn't work. It didn't fit. It didn't fit. What do I want, then? "We were designed to accommodate, remember. Use this strength and experience to help you learn more about yourself and what you really need in life. In a painful experience or in a state of readiness to motivate fear, imagine someone who faced adversity-without overcoming fear, they would not have been successful.

5. Know that failure is inevitable

You're going to fail. The process is only part of it. This will be told to every successful person. However, failure provides insights and corrects the defective ways to address the problem. No professor is as influential as the failure sting. And no lesson better in resilience than the rejection burning. However, you have a vantage that no one else can use as unique information to adjust your strategy and approach the next time around.

You have to choose that your dreams are more important than your fear of failure if you are ready to stop experiencing fear-based lives. Make today the decision to overcome fear and make yourself the happiest, most successful version possible.

The most important lesson we learn in life, for all that we are taught in school, is that which the result of a hard knock-school is. Fear is what moves us. Fear is what moves us. Fear is what keeps us here. Fear is what is reversing us. Fear is what we're afraid of. But the kid inspires us with fear. We are looking for ways to inspire and separate us from this lifelong adversary and friend of ours.

Think of what an education in life really means. Kindly ask yourself — what does it really mean to you?

Is it a good job to get good grades? Will it be a better and more intimate way to know yourself? Is this love? Hope?-Hope? Do you believe? Awareness? What are the things you want to really include in your life— the system is damned? And what are you prepared to do?

You will be on their side every step of your journey fear. You get more accustomed to it, therefore. And it is helpful to know that you learn from fear as much as you learn from anything else regardless of your path. It will shape you, but you will also be able to use it to shape your world.

The Education of Life

We learn the most important lessons of life, from reading, arithmetic learning, analysis of compounds, elements and more: overcoming fear and adversity, rebuilding errors and failures and building rock-solid relations between our personal and professional lives come outside our system. We expect parents, friends, even enemies to glean these things.

But what about when we don't?

We are left to our own faculties, which are often unable or unfamiliar to help us in the real things. You're going to get a great education. No doubt about this. There's no doubt. But where you really win is when you learn to combine your thoughts and actions with emotional intelligence.

This piece by Matt Brubaker and Foster Mobley from the Harvard Business Review takes into account four major ways of fighting fear. It is a good step-by-step process that incorporates emotional understanding and breaks down four parts of fear and how this cycle is evident in our lives:

"Step 1: Recognizing Fear: in the recognition phase, we suggest that people look into their history carefully and examine the choices made by them and the reasons for them."

Step 2: question the fear of better comprehension: evaluate the reality of the situation and look at the cost of fear... consider what if something fails.'

"Step 3: Choose another action course. The matter is to decide next and commit yourselves — to understand what is really important to you.

"Step 4: Acted in a manner that corresponds to your values. Your commitments are the last step.

For fear to be tackled, attributes such as recognition, confrontation and choice of action and engagement are crucial. Our self-confidence, empathy, care for oneself and the bravery to fight fear are revealed. Essential to our living conditions.

Yet we run away from our dreams by so many of us. Our issue is not that we're not courageous, conscious, or thoughtful enough.

Making Your Move

You can try this simple exercise as well:

Take a deep breath and think about the thing that you love most in your life.

It could be your family or your friends, but put it into a distinct bucket for a second to your side. Think about what you're most passionate about, hobby, activity or venture that inspires, inspires, enthuses and lights the fire in you.. What are the colors and meanings of your life?

The things you are dreaming of are calling you to do deeply into your insight, heart and mind..

Now–attempt the easy workout: look back over the previous six months. How many times in that period have you moved in this direction?

Indeed— how far did you really travel if, after a retrospective, you were to measure your progress towards the thing you love?

What if I tell you that you began from the same situation all the good individuals you admire? Not economic status or class, ethnicity or background. I'm not speaking about. I speak of the state of mind and emotion in life. Combat or fly to face your greatest dreams and difficulties.

We either move in the direction of what we want, or we either do not move forward or even retreat. The response to one of the most significant issues of life is never found: what if we really become who are to be?

It's not a matter of wish. In our minds starts want to or hope. Then, we must think that we can do what we want. This is called faith. That is called faith. By supporting our faith with excitement, we have built a strong rock base of emotional well-being. It is doubtful that you can ever do something excellent without that.

The excellent news is— you probably have that already. You have this, you must think and you must be excited. You have that in you.

From this important time — this time of epic life— it's the turning point, whether you live your dreams or are medium-sized. I'm not really talking about sounding dour or pessimistic, actually, far from it. I'm an optimist from outside. I'm also listening to you saying that the next step— the desire and the means of overcoming fear — will make or break you.

Counter-Intuitive Fight

If you are ready to fight — you must first prepare yourself mentally and emotionally to overcome this horrific enemy which threatens to thwart you even before you start. The voice within your head must be overcome and all the following lies be told:

You're not good/talented/able/skilled enough

You're too young or too old

You don't have enough experience

You won't be able to understand what to do with success

You won't be able to grow that business you want so dearly

You're better off trying something different; this is just too tough for you

The list goes on. The list goes on. Please know if you were there before, that I have been and will still be with you. So will the biggest success stories across the history in all fields and industries. Nobody knows for sure if they will ever do it. Our success and our ideas depend on the acceptability, need or want of tens, hundreds and thousands of other people!

And no matter how well-trained or prepared we are on the market, we're never going to know, until we attempt to penetrate. We have to shoot things regardless if our idea is initial or nonoriginal.

Secondly, that is why everything is done. You are prepared to act? You're prepared to go for what you want? Because if you are, you have to reverse your desire, faith and enthusiasm foundations. You don't have to worry what other people think. You must fight to your advantage by using fear. This is how to reach your life's greatest expectations and dreams.

Turning your fear into a superpower

My father has been a waterman warrior open sea,' says Chris Bertish, a big surfer of the wave. "I'm the youngest of three brothers, and I've been unbelievably committed to keep up from an early age. I think I didn't realize that at that time, but it helped me get ridiculously focused.

This focus has led Bertish to apparently superhuman accomplishments. He won the International Mavericks Big Wave Surfing Event on the greatest waves recorded in sport history. He has a 24-hour open ocean stand paddle record in South Africa and is the World Record for 12 hours of Open Ocean Guinea. He has also enjoyed great success as a professional talker / water adventurer traveling the world.

But he thinks everyone can accomplish, well... anything. His device is: dream, see, believe, accomplish. You begin to believe that anything is possible when you hear him talk about it. He has a secret, see. See. A superpower he says we all have, but many of us ignore it. What does this superpower mean? This is fear. It's fear.

"Everyone is afraid, it's natural and normal. People don't realize that you shouldn't be paralyzed by fear. Fear leads you to an increased mental and physical ability to help you overcome the adversity you encounter at that time, "said Bertish.," he said.

You can recognize that, instead of letting fear hinder you, it is actually there for you to help. Fear is the trigger to prepare Bertish for her best performance.

"What fear does your body do to ask yourself?"That is what Bertish says. "It sends endorphins into your body and sends your system with adrenaline, and it pumps your heart faster, shooting your whole body with oxygen.. It strengthens you three times more than usual and makes it possible for your mind to process information more quickly than usually, "says Mr Bertish.

"To be afraid is to say: this is the perfect moment to do what you try. Actually, your body prepares you for a positive result. Once you really understand this, you can do things that are extraordinary to most people.

"If you take out fear and see what your body is doing, you can recognize that basically it's setting you up to do what you are trying to do," he says. "Fear says: this is the perfect time to do what you want to do. Actually, your body prepares you for a positive result. You may learn to manage this once you really understand that fear is an emotion like any other. Then you can do things that are extraordinary for the majority of people, "says Bertish.

This description of fear makes sense when it comes to a man who waves as large as five-story houses for fun. Bertish uses fear as its connection with the flow situation which sportsmen claim can perform at its peak. He has learnt to usefully handle and treat his fear. "I see fear as an unbelievably positive thing which is essential and necessary for all that I do. If I'm in a state of fear, I try to make the most of my experience. I use it under pressure to make fast and efficient decisions. I can take the correct decisions very quickly by using all the knowledge and experience that I have in the past, coupled with the physical fitness that gives me confidence and backed by the powerful tools I received right now! This helped me to succeed and to survive certain intense situations on the ocean.

While Bertish uses fear for handling lives and death, he believes that this physical boost, which is superhuman, can help you everywhere in your life. "In general, your body pumps you up with a natural enhancer of performance. In fact, that's what is going on inside you. Fear allows you to work beyond your absolute peak. And it's natural! And it's natural!"It's laughing. "It's incredible. It's the secret that's best kept.

Naturally, you still have to train, prepare and train in the time. "It is this which gives you the trust to know that you can move it to the next level," Bertish says. "Within the ever changing and deadly environment in which I play and compete, that belief that I know you're physically and mentally ready is crucial and essential."

What about Bertish next? In addition to speaking at conferences worldwide, he plans a custom-built stand-up paddle board across the Atlantic. You can be sure that he will do it once he puts his mind on something.

Chapter 10
Communication: As A
Means Of Relation

Why Is Communication So Important To Human Life?

Communication is a process by which people send and receive information. People do not only interact face-to-face with others, but also by providing data on the Internet and printed products like books and journals. Many think that the importance of communication is like breathing. In fact, communication promotes the spread of information and interactions among individuals.

Communication first enables individuals to disseminate understanding and data. Authors, for instance, write books to give knowledge to the world and teachers to their students. Also, friends and colleagues discuss their ideas and businesses with their subsidiaries and customers exchange information. Furthermore, the advent of the Internet makes it easier and faster for people around the globe not nur to have better access to knowledge and information in all fields. Therefore, without communication there can be no sharing of knowledge and information process. In consequence, companies can't work and humanity will fall into the abyss of ignorance.

Communication is, moreover, the basis of all relations between human beings. At first, strangers begin to talk and meet, and when they have a greater contact and communication, the connections are created. Communication enables individuals express their thoughts and emotions and it simultaneously enables us to comprehend others ' emotions and thoughts. This creates affection or hatred towards others and creates beneficial or negative relations.

Communication certainly plays an important role in human existence. It helps not only to promote data and knowledge sharing, but also to build relationships with others. Therefore, it can not be underestimated the significance of communication. We interact with many, including our families, friends, peers and even strangers, every day. We should learn how to effectively communicate in order to improve our lives.

Communication abilities are important for a happy and successful life. Effective communication covers honesty, trust, charity, binding, sharing, caring and friendship among different types of communities, religions and individuals. Effective communication skills align all people in a single direction that stimulates social, cultural and economic growth. Therefore, in life the abilities to communicate are significant.

Now, let's learn in details:

Communication skills are the presentation of your character:

The ability to communicate is evidence of what as a human being. It's the way you're behaving and talking to individuals. It's like affecting individuals around you.

For instance, a professional communicator or a good person knows how to communicate in specific situations with different types of people. You understand how to speak to children, relatives, families, friends and strangers. It's about regard in all these instances.

It shows how good you are as a individual when you talk humbly with all of the individuals. In which you do not only communicate humbly for profit, but because it is your nature and nature. you do so instead.

Many individuals interact differently with everyone, for instance, communicating with the wealthy with humility and respect, but with the bad bad. This is their nature and personality. They communicate with the people who meet their standards in humility and respect. And there are reasons behind that.

So respectful and humble communication is a skill of communication which shows the good / bad components of human nature. And it's difficult to make an impact on the world without good character and live a happy life. That is why in a life that relies on humility and respect for others good communication skills are important.

Communication skills create and strengthen friendships:

A tongue can simultaneously make thousands of friends and enemies. This is how and when you're using it. We forget words and vocabulary in anger, for example. We don't mind such a rude situation with other people. We don't care. Father, mother, true friend, wife, child, customer or somewhere else in anger don't care about us. And in anger, we use the words from inside that hurt people.

This is why anger, aggressional and rugged communication is a poor communication skill, which can turn a foe into an enemy or an honest friend. Therefore, in negative situations it is important to stay calm.

You read, write, work and drive or whatever you do, for example. Someone has gone a long way and distracted you unintentionally like playing music loudly, jam traffic, ticket counter line, high sugar tea, etc. The poor communicator gets upset and frustrates the words. The other person was also angry at the same time. It doesn't matter whether or not they understand one another. However, they will begin to fight, debate and blame each other for the reason. The discussion can become a larger battle within a few minutes.

Now, what the cause of this fight?

The reason for this is a lack of patience. Communication patience is the greatest skill, and not half of the people on the planet. It seems like animals are wearing shoes and clothes, driving cars, and working in the office. I know it's hard to keep calm all the time. This is a test, however, for a good communicator and a good man. When someone has passed the test, he / she is a good communicator.

The patience of communication teaches you how to speak and when. If someone is mad, you just want to listen to me. You don't have to respond quickly. Just look at the moment and the situation.

The key ability to communicate is listening. It's all silence. Silence has words of its own. That's also why I'm trying to be a good listener. It's all about receiving and filtering information through facts and information. Don't talk if someone doesn't ask for a reply. But if you ask rudely / badly, it means you need love and trust.

In this situation you need to communicate softly and humbly. In this way, you're going to earn respect for them and others. It will demonstrate the quality of your character. You're going to build friendship and partnership.

I therefore think it is important to have good communication skills, based on patience, observation and analysis, for a happy and prosperous life.

Communication skills are very significant in career development:

Communication skills contribute to the goals of career development. New learning and technical / non-technical expertise of every type required skills in communication such as listening, writing and questions. Communication abilities such as self-exposure, methods of study presentation and experiences before the employer and interviewers.

Body languages, dresses, style of walking, eating and drinking, contact with the eye, hands control... all about us. all about us. This is why it is important for every professional to improve communication skills. How we talk to your co-workers, students and the working world, etc. helps us to achieve support, appreciation and respect.

You have heard or learned that it earns respect. We need more communication skills than money to earn that respect from team members, classmates, bosses, seniors, society, friends and the families. Therefore, good communication skills representing us what we are and are made of are important to us.

Communication skills are important in business:

The ability to communicate helps the business in many ways. It contributes to marketing, sales, management of people and the development of long-term customer relations. The way that businesses / sellers / teams communicate throughout the purchase process changes sales.

Efficient message, words, phrases, colours, characters, objects used in advertising, for example, have a positive effect on potential customers.

Everything communicates with marketing, such as product design, company logo, landing page message, product description, applications choices, everything necessary to sell and buy is communication. And it's going to operate if it's efficient.

Communication skills are important to become a leader:

Leaders tend to develop a positive attitude, change the mentality of the company, push the group of people into the right direction, build teams to reach certain goals, inspire the speed and accuracy of the business plan and lead people through examples. Communication skills play an important role in all these things.

It is difficult for an individual leader to have a positive attitude if he does not communicate positively. Through communication, they must define goals, directions and ideas You can use digital content, blogs, social media, meetings, seminars, speeches, discussion groups and so on. Effective and motivational communication plays an important role in all these things. And it's hard to gain trust and support from the society if presentation, discourse, plan, application or guidelines are not effective.

The administration defines the law, for example. But people do not personalize the language they choose to define the law. Many people do not understand the vocabulary of law / government. And if you can't understand it, then how can you comply with the law? This is why it is not only important for the government, but for every organization, leaders must communicate effectively and show things.

Communication skill helps to become educated:

As I mentioned above, it is important to have communication skills in order to learn any skills. But let's get it deeper now.

The abilities to communicate assistance to be trained. You have not been taught a degree, diploma or technical knowledge. It's evidence that you visited the university and did the course. It does not imply you know the organisational plans and are sufficiently trained to manage them.

The manner in which you interact with a distinct public in distinct favorable and adverse circumstances and techniques is evidence of your knowledge / idea / principles / law / issues / topic.

There are many people who do not attend college and university, but they are educated and experienced in the way they communicate.

I know you've been to government offices thousands of times. You witnessed how you communicated with those officers and bureaucrats. For instance, if a subdivision judge and a extremely qualified public worker interact rudely, comport poorly with people, the amount of education and understanding is shown. There are exceptions in certain circumstances.

You've also seen that many doctors, officials, officials, even peon leaders communicate very badly with the poor. The law and order are worse than good in this situation. Only through communication. This is why communication abilities assist us learn.

We know others when we hear patiently. When we communicate with love and grace, we are able to understand the issues of the citizens, and this is how to help others. So I think it's important to have good communication skills in order to be really educated.

So, in short, I can tell that communication skills assist us not only to live for ourselves but also to others gladly, graciously, and successfully. It helps build a favorable atmosphere and enables large stuff.

No one cares today about how much cash you gain, how wealthy you are. Without strong communication abilities you're unable to gain regard for your children, relatives, family and community.

Efficient communication is just as essential to the body as nutrition. For the behavior, everyone will remind you. And abilities in communication educate us how to act like human beings.

You can understand and enjoy distinct incredible data about the significance of communication.

1. Importance of Communication in Life

Communication plays an important role in making interaction quicker in our daily interaction. We need to communicate as quickly as possible in order to make life easier. We are one way of solving every problem as a social being. We also need to improve our know-how in each industry as the globe has evolved. You can't even think about some development without communication.

2. Importance of Communication in an Organization

An enterprise communication performs an efficient part in motivating and inspirational. Communication provides brave support to distribute every effective skill in a foundation. In an organisation, it is called efficient communication.

The employer must understand how the worker performs the work. For this, every industry in the base must be communicated by the employer. An organisation will be damaged if the work is not done properly. This could lead to long-term problems for the organisation. If an employee frequently communicates with all industry of the company, the issue for which work is not done frequently can be found. The communication will also help the company find the right solution to the problem.

3. Importance of Communication in Business

What is corporate communication skills? Business means negotiation in order to achieve your objectives. Owners often need to expand their sales to earn more income. The communication shows the proprietor how sales in other nations can be improved.

If the company maintains a good communication with the culture of a foreign country, it can benefit from certain abilities that will certainly contribute to every facet of its business results. The following functions are provided to help develop a large business market.

- Successful Brand messaging
- Great team relationships
- Preventing confrontment
- The inspiration for an innovative promotion

4. Importance of Communication in Society

In the aspect of our human beings, the importance of communication in society can be defined. We must communicate regularly every day to reside in community.

Nobody can talk to you about anything. So what is it going to feel? We have to talk and maintain communication with others as a human being. We can't resist it as a partnership.

5. Importance of Communication in Management

There is a certain management communications procedure. We are undoubtedly following these procedures.

To manage diverse types of works.

We have to manage others for a desired opts.

We manage our home task by ourselves

In every field of life, managerial work lies. You should remember that in managerial work, communication plays a crucial role.

6. Importance of Communication in Education

Education means learning. Teachers and students need to communicate with each other to ensure proper learning, but communication is a must to develop students ' speaking and listening skills.

We all know that the student of today is a future leader or speaker. There will be no hesitation, discomfort and lack of trust if you are learning to communicate with the teacher properly. Communication also contributes to becoming a friendly person who is truly important. Students can gain skills for development and professionalism in their attitude by learning correct communication.

7. In Transportation

The main issues in the development of any region are communication and transport. We can see that off-road facilities are much more developed in developed countries than in undeveloped countries. Not only routes, when we look at their train and plane transport, but also the boat we can see that they use their communication system as advantageously as possible.

Most developed countries have sent satellites for transport development. They connect to the satellite to keep their root of the plane safe and secure. Their infrastructure for transport is therefore far safer than developing and undeveloped countries.

8. In leadership skill

One day you want to be a big leader? Then try to communicate as closely as possible with the public. The best way to achieve leadership is through communication.

You will be able to understand people's demand if you communicate with others. You'll also come to an understanding of what the subject is and is the best thing to attain sophisticated management. What's the greatest scenario?

9. Importance of communication in Social Media

Social media is currently a platform to express your views. Like, anything related to this article can be commented on right now. Think of a problem you are faced with, and you requested online help, and a solution is found. We are all connected together. The effective things of ICT and the IT world are already an effective matter.

There are currently many social media. Communication is the main requirement to connect with others in these social media.

10. Importance of Communication in Technology

Since many countries send spacecraft to explore the cosmos, they must maintain a relationship regularly with the cosmonaut. In this sector too, modern communication systems play a crucial role.

Like space science, we have to connect with existing technologies. Communication is a better way for all of us to spread new technology.

Hope that in every step of life you understand the importance of communication. You can't express your opinion to others if you don't communicate. Yes, for those who don't want to communicate with others, this is a big problem. But try to communicate and give others the opportunity to communicate with you.

Chapter 11
Loving What Earns You A Living: Job

When you are too long in the same workplace, you may have lost your passion for your job. Here are some symptoms which show that you don't love your job anymore. You may start complaining about your workload. You may even start to "hate' your employer. There are many things you don't like about your company, such as company policies, medical benefits, remuneration package, working environment, etc. You may not agree with me. But let's read on.

Many people say that they love their jobs, but sometimes they don't show it. They don't show their commitment and they don't take accountability. For those fresh graduates, at the initial stage, they could not do enough for their jobs. They might strive hard to achieve their employers' expectations. However, when they have reached certain level, they start to take their jobs for granted. They just treat their jobs as a "vehicle" for them to generate income.

In common, most of the working adults go through this process. When they were courting their jobs, they talked all things nice about what they were doing and they promised their commitment to it. However, when the duration is too long, they have nothing but they keep complaining about their jobs. They even threaten their bosses to leave their jobs! Some of them make resignation as a tool to request for salary increment.

They don't realize that their jobs can work wonders. They don't know that their jobs can change their entire life. In fact, their jobs provide great satisfaction in their life but they are not aware of it. May be when their jobs have gone, then only they will start appreciating their work. They have forgotten that their jobs are responsible for the food on their table, the clothes they wear and for the welfare of their home sweet home.

Having positive mindset from time to time is important no matter how many years you are in the workplace. Even we are from different industries and different lines, we need to cherish our jobs. We get paid by our employers every month for our services. Hence, we need to provide the best to our organizations. Our contribution is essential in assisting the organizations to achieve great success. In return, we are rewarded. We gain financial stability.

I hope that this statement will always be remembered. "Take good care of your job and you will be well looked after."

Ask Yourself: "Do I Love my Job "

You spend most of your day working more than you can spend at home and with your family.

The job has become your home, your collaborators are your brothers, and your "securities" who have knowledge of what is always best for you are your parents.

And again, you ask yourself, "Is this what I really want? Am I glad at work? Is it worth all the work I've done during the week?."

Let's sit back for a second, visualize and begin to think about your day at work.

How can I know that I love what I do, and that's what I love?

You Love Mondays

Sometimes in your lives you should have had the Monday Blues to know what I'm talking about (if you had never had the Monday Blues, well, you're a lucky few in the world). Yes, it's Monday blues, but if we look at the people that live in this state of mind, everything begins on Sunday afternoon where "the weekend is gone, I must work tomorrow..." is the only thing they can think of.

Check out somebody who comes to work with the Monday blues. You're never happy, you can't tolerate the Morning chats, you've always ready a coffee cup before you say good morning and you have a problem trying to smile because it feels like a terrible punishment with certain particular circumstances in which a person reminds you how many' day: heures: minutes.'

You don't have to worry about the Monday Blues a minute if you love your job. You will wake up to work with this positive attitude. Mondays are quite like any day of the weekend for you. Monday's Walk through the park, a new day to explore, socialize and take advantage of new adventures. You're a Monday person if you look at yourself!

Productivity

Many struggle trying to be productive throughout the day and many get to fail this task day in/day out since they don't love what they do.

True, they get to fulfill their tasks and duties, but with bare minimum effort and quality. How can you assess if you are one of the low productive individuals at work? Take a closer look at what you do and specify the time it took you to accomplish it, in comparison to the time it should have been done. If this is a recurring step, then you are out of focus since your work is not interesting enough for you, affecting your time management, and feeling stuck in a task that is a never ending endeavor. An additional thing that can help you find out how productive you are relates to always trying to find something that keeps you away from work such as sleeping, eating, internet surfing, mobile gaming, social media, etc.

BUT, if you are a person that multi-tasks, gets the job done right from the first time (Not always! We are all human), always involved in helping others to do well, and have the spirit of "what can I pick up next?", then you my friend, is one productive person at work. In addition, if you get to leave work with the personal satisfaction of achieving & conquering new obstacles throughout the day, then I hold out my hat for you, cause not only your are a productive person, but a daily achiever.

The Extra Mile

Each individual has a comfort zone. Imagine your comfort zone as your home couch, with a coffee table filled with your perfect meals or fast food, and your favorite TV series airing all day long (or your favorite books in case you are not into TV). So if we need to add the Extra Mile to the above, then it's like having your mother (when you were a kid) turning off the TV, taking away all the food, and asking you to go clean up your room or you will never even see daylight again. Tough, right? Well, nothing comes easy, especially when trying to shoot outside your comfort zone.

BUT, if you are that person who always gets to achieve more than what is expected from you, always rewarded as employee of the month/year, getting bonuses for amazing work done, shooting new innovative ideas, then you are the person who aims high beyond their job description. In reference to the example above, before watching tv, you clean your room, do the dishes, take out the garbage, all done before turning on the TV, and by that keep mother happy.

"Procrastination" is not a word that can be found in your dictionary.

I Do What I Love, I Love What I Do

What do you call "a paid position of regular employment"?

A Job.

You refer to it as a daily process that you can't get rid off but you wish you can. You eventually find yourself working to sustain yourself. It is not "You Live to work" anymore as much as "You work to live". You find yourself losing passion for what you do, your mental state is blocked, and eventually you are in a lock-down and so deep it is very hard to change or do anything that can turn the wheel to your favor (It's not the end of the world still!).

BUT, if you are passionate about what you do, you stopped counting working hours, you find the day passing like a breeze with all the stress and tasks you have, and eventually when asked "What do you

do?" you reply back "What I love"... instead of saying "my job"..
Then I applaud you for finding your passion in life whereas many
are still searching.

Take this article as a challenge to find if you enjoy what you do. Ask
yourself what are the signs above that fit your profile and which
don't. Get to assess your situation cause you, especially you, deserve
to be happy. So, what are you waiting for?

According to none other than Forbes, not liking your job is one of
the major causes for economic slumps!

Add to this the shocking results from a recent (anonymously
collected) Gallup poll that show approximately 85 percent of
workers worldwide hate their job and their boss and our ongoing
economic struggles suddenly make sense.

With more than one billion workers worldwide, the fact that just 15
percent do more than tolerate their day-to-day work lives may sound
depressing. But the truth is, there has never been a better moment
than now to understand the significance – the vital importance – of
learning to love your job.

What Does It Look Like to Love Your Job?

In its most mundane, you want to appear regularly and largely on
time when you love your career. You are happy and happy
throughout the business day and use your working hours to perform
more than well.

You look for a small amount to contribute when you love your work, and you try not to add extra work to the plates of your colleagues by not pulling your weight.

When you love your job, you may be willing to deal with difficult or additional tasks, arrive early or remain late at a time of "crunch," lend an assistant colleague and work hard to keep critical talks friendly and constructive.

If you love your employment, you will study yourself as your own—because it is in your mind and heart!-as a result of your profits versus costs, company culture and future of your field!

These are the things we love if it's a task, a pet, a plant, a person or something.

Think of something or someone you love and how you speak and behave. If you have trouble visualizing what it would be like to love your job, Swap the rest now and pretend instead that it's your job. You now know what your job looks like.

Is it Really Possible to Love Your Work?

Maybe you read this right now and don't really like your work today. Perhaps you are looking for new work in a different role or industry in order to connect with your passion. You might have had a number of jobs that you didn't love and start to wonder whether "loving your work" is an urban myth. It's not and it's not. Even people who are genuinely in love with their jobs can be exposed to overwork or stagnation because there are no new opportunities. Poor management, tough employees and a changing economy can sometimes make the romance shrink.

All of this is the best place to start learning to fall in love all over again with your work, wherever you are. In other words, you need to fix what is broken, mend what is exhausted or diminishing, make personal and professional changes or perhaps return to higher education or further training or certification before you fall into love with your present job or find your new job to love. You need to do something.

This can take time and by nature most of us will not be patient if we want to change our lives. But it will really pay off to take the time to identify what doesn't work in your current job or field, make adjustments or even map a new course for a job that can never quickly jump.

Start By Loving Yourself and Loving Your Job Will Follow

When things get harder at work, things get harder both inside and at home. You may feel physically tired or even sick, especially on Monday or just after a long vacation!

Maybe with your partner and family you will have more tense words at home. At night, you may feel restless and unable to sleep deep and relax. Work stress can penetrate all areas of your life, worsening it until it feels like the whole world conspires against you.

This is not. It is not. But unwittingly you may have begun to conspire against yourself, feed on a steady diet of critical words and thoughts, make comparisons with other–happier–colleagues, believe that you are too old or too stuck or too dependent on a stream of income for you to ever love your job.

It's a good time to support your health, relationships, self-assessments and quality of life in other areas so you won't go downhill in a disappointing career. There are resources available if you want career counseling. The same applies to relationship counselling to help you and your family cope.

If this benefit is provided in your company you can take stock, rest, get medical attention if you want it and eventually regroup and return in combat form again. You can benefit from short sabbatical training.

All New Growth Comes From Facing Existing Challenges

Old Steps

You start to take steps that are aligned with your priority when you decide that loving your job is a priority.

Although they can't speak about it so openly, many happy workers hate their jobs today. You can finally learn to love your job with patience, courage and willingness to change.

Why Is It Important To Do What You Love?

We've all heard the saying' do what you love and you'll get the money.' But unfortunately it's not so easy and finding a way to do what you love and earn enough to support yourself and your family can, with the rising cost of living, be a difficult challenge. Certainly, we must all make sacrifices at some point in life, but happiness should not be one of them. It should be a priority to find a way of getting happy in your career, since if you don't feel happy at work, then probably not happy at home, which can affect your environment. People that do what they like are more productive lives. They live happier. Here are ten reasons why what you love for a life should be done:

- If you are glad at work you are feeling good about yourself and are more likely to find opportunities. You're more self-esteem. You will have more energy, which will further develop your career.
- Everybody goes through tough times in their careers, and if you like what you do, you will most likely go through the tough times instead of feeling overwhelmed and giving up. You are not motivated and proactive. You will always be motivated and inspired to continue to work.
- Everybody goes through tough times in their careers, and if you like what you do, you will most likely go through the tough times instead of feeling overwhelmed and giving up. You are not motivated and proactive. You will always be motivated and inspired to continue to work.
- By being pleased you can drive business, gain more customers, achieve goals, etc. that will result in a well-deserved pay rise. you will have more earning potential
- Your general health is improved by people who do not like their work, who may experience increased blood pressure, headaches, stress, etc. You will have a better overall health if you enjoy your work

- Because a positive person is able to take a stance, your colleagues will receive more respect from you, which makes your working environment much more happy

- You're going to have a more happy home rather than coming home stressed and unhappy, for your family and friends.

- If you work you will have a higher production rate and will be able to meet all the challenges of your job. You will be more productive.

- You'll improve mental health By providing meaning and purpose that can be related to the psychological well-being, what you love improves mental health

- You will serve other customers and consumers who love their jobs naturally. You're also going to do a better job! It's really going hand in hand!!

Love Your Job and It Will Love You in Return

If you are working more and enjoying it less and at the same time dreading every work day and going to your work place, then maybe it is high time for you to consider other career choices that life has to offer. A person certainly spends a substantial portion of life at the workplace and it is vital to keep this time as personally and professionally rewarding as possible. Every single day, people are making radical turns in their careers. Opportunities to exist but will these changes really make us contented and happy as soon as we get there? Here are tips for you to start loving your job.

Always keep in mind that your work should not define you, but how you do the job does. There is definitely a lot to be spoken for a person's attitude. Any task can be done well- done with care and compassion. A person's attitude at the workplace and the way he treats people (even one's mood) can oftentimes go unnoticed. These factors may have that profound influence on the individuals you are working with. There may be times when you can't do anything with the situation but we can always choose how we live it.

Stop focusing yourself on how money and how much financial gain you can get from your work. Money is something that will never be enough so quit utilizing it as an excuse. Whatever you are taking with you during paydays, there are things that you could do if you had more. Track all your expenses in a week. Knowing where your money goes will help you refocus your spending habit on the things that you really need. Getting paid is only a small fraction of what you do, your job should be looked at as something more than a paycheck to make it more fulfilling.

Find the significance in the things that you do. This may ask you to think big but is definitely something doable. Take some time to ponder on the things that you do at work. Is it an essential service that you are providing to clients? Perspective plays a major role in attaining personal fulfillment and that sense of well-being.

Ask yourself what your job is worth. If you're job changes you into a person whom you don't know anymore, then consider probable reasons. Do you like the person that is becoming when you are performing your work? Sometimes, it's not a new job that you need but a new direction.

Asking yourself reasons why you choose this job doesn't necessarily mean that you are dissatisfied. It only means that you're becoming more aware of yourself. This awareness may be the key for you to love your job more.

Chapter 12
The Final Chapter: Live!!!

Good life can mean for everyone something else. There is, however, still a general understanding of the implications of the idea for most people living in the modern world. Good life is a series of satisfactions in its simplest shape, which only increases with time.

The good life is that every morning I want to get out of bed, happy to take whatever it takes each day. The material possessions or sensations artificially induced have nothing to do with them. The good life is based on your compassionate actions, personal goals and the legacy you decide to leave behind due to your mark on the world around you.

When the private jet was off and Kanye West had made his debut on the singular "The Good Life" choir, who could forget that episode of the Entourage? What he was talking about was not money that the characters got, but celebration for their success as a team.

Too many people get tangled in the past and in the future, wondering what will happen to themselves and considering the "if it is." They become stupid at the little moments that the building blocks of time unknowingly are. After all, time is indeed our greatest benefit to living the entire life.

After all, this world still is a miracle to all our sciences; beautiful, magical and more, to anyone that wants to think about it. Carlyle Thomas

Here are several simple ways to live the good life.

1. Slow Down

Precision, awareness and happiness immediately decrease. The difference between doing things and doing things effectively is great.

2. Appreciate Life's Simple Pleasures.

The best of life is really free. The most simple pleasures of a life can only be bought if the mind is aware of their arrival, from a quiet sea sunset to sleeping during a rainy day.

3. Foster and Nurture Relationships.

A happy and pleasant life is a life shared with the people you like most. Treat your friends as you want to be treated. Treat your relationships.

4. Be Self Sufficient.

Depending on others, only anxiety and frustration are caused by your own peace. Use your freedom and autonomy. The only person who can really tell you what you want or need is yourself at the end of the day.

5. Learn About Different Things.

The day you stop learning is, as so many great men have said in the past, the day you die. It is an opportunity to learn about the life you want to achieve or the person you want to be every day. Continue to explore and inquire. A jack of all businesses is much more equipped than just a master.

6. Focus on Your Passions.

Every day you love to do your passion, because it gives you a sense of value and satisfaction. You can focus on your true purpose of life, which is the key to real wealth on this earth. Use your passion as productive and universal as possible and you will find out why your major efforts and goals lie behind it.

7. Travel to Distant Places.

Mankind was blessed with a lovely place to live. Experience all the wonders of nature and culture it has to offer. In this world, there are places that open your mind to realities that you have never imagined in the wildest of your dreams. These truths inject new and healthy perspectives into your consciousness.

8. Talk to Strangers.

Meet new people like you and in all ways you could have imagined different from you. This will assist you in taking on the gift of individuality and understanding the role you play in society. Understanding these people will increase your understanding of how the world works and how people create their experiences.

9. Exercise Your 5 Senses.

Eyesight, hearing, smell, flavor and feeling. Everyone gives you the opportunity to reward personal experiences, so use them to make you really understand what life means. See the best things, hear the best sounds, taste the best food, smell the best fragrances and touch the nicest tits.

10. Use What You Have.

Success is not an unlimited resource by-product. When the limits of the available resources are extended, success happens. Don't concentrate on that you don't have, concentrate on what you have and how you can get the rest.

12. Assist Others.

What's going on is happening. You don't know what kind of fulfillment and security you can achieve by helping other people more and more.

13. Be Clear on Your Goals.

The sky is the limit, but to reach your goals, it is necessary that your whole heart and soul believes it crystal clear. If you don't know what you want and don't think you have the necessary information to get it, you'll never get where you want to go.

14. Make a Decision.

You waste your time and opportunity to make a decision every time you wait. Stop being indecisive and listen to your intestines. Choices are how we learn how to build the life that we have always dreamed of effectively.

15. Practice General Time Management.

Trying to meet your objectives without planning a little time is like sailing the open ocean without a map. Sure it's fun, but you have to remember at the end of the day why you're out there.

16. Be Spontaneous.

Opportunity knocks at times that are unforeseen. Make sure that you have sufficient flexibility to respond to your schedule.

Be spontaneous and walk away from your comfort zone at all times. Experience new things that you might have been afraid of but always wanted to try to satisfy you. At first glance, the most euphoric activities are unbelievably frightening.

17. Be present.

One of the biggest problems in this world is that they are trapped in the past and in the future, that by accepting the moment right before their eyes they refuse to take control of their lives.

They constantly worry about other things; there's their body, but elsewhere's their mind. It will make you a much happier and inspired person, be present in every moment.

18. Think More, Talk Less.

The more you think and speak, the more you learn and the less you miss. The more you think. And make sure that you do so with value, significance and conviction when you talk.

19. Own Up to Your Actions.

Judge yourself by how you fulfill your duties and pledges. Either you own your actions or you own your actions. Keep your hands on the wheel and stop teaching, always remember that you're on the driver sit.

20. Keep Your Promises.

This does not ensure solitude and failure. Stay true to your word because this is the basis of your character and how you'll always be remembered.

21. Always Find the Positive Lesson.

There is a positive lesson for every negative result. It's the key to grandeur to remember them.

22. Forget Perfection, Find Satisfaction.

There's no so perfect thing, there's only awareness. The idea is based on the definition of yourself. You are looking for things that satisfy your individual wants and needs rather than always looking for perfection.

23. Work Hard.

To be lazy and to do the bare minimum only ensures mediocrity and unhappiness. Work hard every day to get closer to your goal.

We all have to work to live, so why not have the best possible fun with that life-consuming activity? Make sure your work drains your energy but also that you feel that you use it well.

24. Sleep Well.

An inefficient and unfortunate tired mind. Without rest no one can do the best they can.

25.Laugh.

As the good old-fashioned saying goes, the more people laugh, the more people live. Stop taking life so seriously and realize that all the nervousness or discomfort that make you really can only make you laugh.

26. Be Here Now.

You can use the time right now, but you like it. Life's right now. Don't just miss it. Don't miss it. It is a whole world that is waiting for your own wishes to take shape.

27. Improve your posture.

Did you know your posture and your body language shapes not only how people view you, but how you feel? If you're not persuaded, watch this TED talk.

28. Find the time for what you want to do.

Many of us constantly complain that we have not enough time or that we are too busy to do / do things. What we need to realize is that we are in the first place in such situations. If you are trapped in a job, are you taking action to get out of the situation? If you are, then pleading shouldn't waste time. What do you complain about when you're not?

29. Don't chase money for the sake of money.

It is important to have money in life, but only because it allows us to chase what we want in life. You only get a life, and when you're six feet on the ground, money isn't good.

30. Overcome laziness.

Have you big objectives and dreams? Stop making changes just because you would like to watch television? After a few attempts, you leave? A little tiredness here and there is natural, but you probably need to work on overcoming the laziness if you look year after year and don't see any changes.

31. Analyze your weaknesses.

One of the hardest thing for people in terms of their own weaknesses is to be objective. Of course, we tend to rationalize things that we're not good at or that we think we're better than we are. You can take active steps in order to work on yourself when you recognize your weaknesses and understand how they hold you back.

32. Constantly work on improving yourself.

You will not meet your goals if you do not do something to improve yourself every day.

33. Master the art of persuasion.

Not to manipulate others, but to manage your fate.

34. Stop trying to please everyone.

It's a great way to make sure you never do any remarkable things.

35. Understand that personality traits aren't static.

While we may all have certain natural genetic and environmental inclinations and gifts, everything changes. Everything is changing. If the aspects of your personality are stopped, whether their laziness, social awkwardness or mediocre intelligence, know that all of these are improvements if you are willing to work on them, rather than accept them as unchanging personality characteristics.

36. Simplify.

The more glad you are, the less you need to be happy.

37. Surround yourself with the type of people you'd want to be.

You're the average of your five nearest friends, there's a saying. While this is not a scientific fact, it is a useful exercise of thought. You will also become negative if you constantly spend time with negative people. You will find your own dreams slipping away if you are time with people without ambition. On the other hand, you're set for success by being surrounded by wonderful people who want the same things you want in life.

38. Design your ideal life.

It's easy to live with the car driver if you don't know what you want. Your first step is to understand what is in life you want. If you want a good framework for doing this, read Tim Ferriss's 4-hour work week.

39. Make a plan to attain your ideal life and execute.

You're going to be given nothing. You will end up on the track in MegaCorp's exciting career by moving paper from one account to the next, if you wait to "see your way" in life. There is no good reason to go through life without end once you're out of school.

40. Stop giving up. Stop giving up.

Have you ever heard of the man who was deserted in the story (urban myth?)? Half a mile from a large oasis town was found. The purpose of this story is to show how dangerous it is to quit. Things will always be difficult until they improve, but if you quit before you see them all the way through, you never know how close you were to achieve your targets.

41. Block out haters.

Building criticism is one thing, but know that if you do great things there you will appeal to haters who want to make criticism. Haters and commentary on Youtube are frequently available to you. Don't personally take your comments and don't get sucked into flames.

42. Accept constructive criticism.

Simultaneously, haters can be good because they may be right sometimes. Our weakness is shown by Haters. If you feel the sting of cognitive dissonance you probably recognize legitimate criticism-you wish to dismiss the thought because it comes from someone who is critic of you, but you can't help shaking that stomach. Instead of entering this feeling, agree that you may be wrong and try to improve yourself so that in the future you will not make the same mistake.

43. Be your own film's hero.

Does life feel mischievous, happy, desperate? Are you feeling stuck in a rut that doesn't leave? Your own film is a hero, you know how to get out. Claim you're the hero in a blockbuster in Hollywood. In every movie the hero is down, with no way out, but always finds a way to overcome the odds. There is a point here. You are a tough place and now it's your job to overcome the odds and come out above–because it's in the script. Pretends you're that hero. Pretend you've been followed by a documentary team, and one day your children's children will see what you did. Want to see a hero overcoming the odds, or a loser playing the victim? The hero does not overcome the chances of watching TV 5 hours a day the last time I checked. Do what is needed, regardless of how difficult it is.

44. Eat, drink, be joyful.

Unbelievable food, great company and engrossing conversation–at least not in this lifetime, it gets little better than that. Enjoy those happy moments and do them as often as possible.

45. Remember one day you will die.

In his now renowned speech at Stanford in 2005, Steve Jobs talks about that. The Dalai Lamai, to quote. Do we live as if we never will die, then we never die?